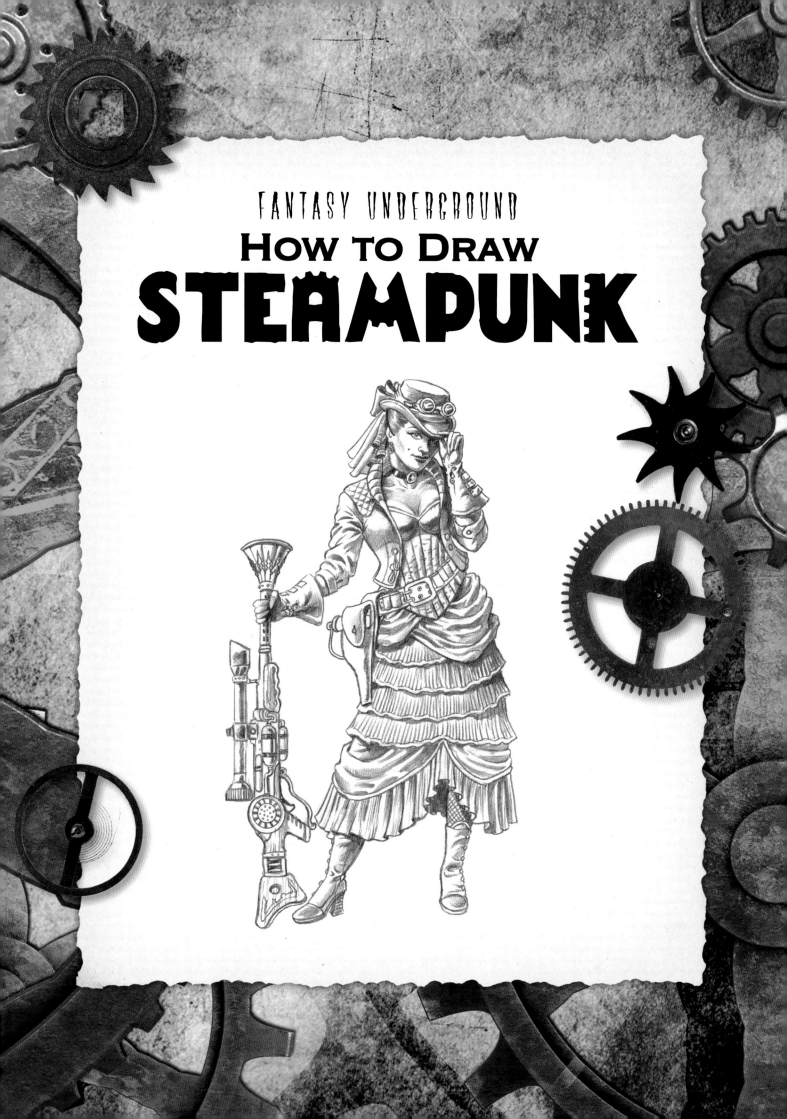

FANTASY UNDERGROUND
How to Draw
STEAMPUNK

This library edition published in 2014 by Walter Foster Publishing,
a Division of the Quayside Publishing Group.
Walter Foster Library
3 Wrigley, Suite A
Irvine, CA 92618

Additional photography: All in One Computer (page 33): Photograph used with permission,
courtesy Sean Slattery, The Steampunk Workshop. The Cleric Weapon (page 37), The Whole 9
Yards Goggles (page 82), Stitch the Steampug (page 128): Photographs used with permission,
courtesy Joey Marsocci and Allison DeBlasio, Dr. Grymm Laboratories. The Grand Experiment
(page 45): Photograph used with permission, courtesy Steve Brook, Steampunk Fabricators. The
Eye of the Nautilus Old Pocket Watch Lace Choker (page 72): Photograph used with permission,
courtesy Amanda Scrivener, Professor Maelstromme. Instructional step-by-step text by Bob Berry.

Distributed in the United States and Canada by
Lerner Publisher Services
241 First Avenue North
Minneapolis, MN 55401 U.S.A.
www.lernerbooks.com

First Library Edition

Library of Congress Cataloging-in-Publication Data

Marsocci, Joey.
  How to draw steampunk / illustrated by Bob Berry ; written by Joey Marsocci & Allison
DeBlasio. -- Library edition.
      pages cm. -- (Fantasy underground)
ISBN 978-1-93958-122-8
1. Fantasy in art. 2. Steampunk culture. 3. Drawing--Technique. I. Berry, Bob, 1953- illustrator.
II. DeBlasio, Allison. III. Title.
  NC825.F25M37 2014
  743'.87--dc23
                                                                                        2013025180

012014
18376

9 8 7 6 5 4 3 2 1

FANTASY UNDERGROUND

How to Draw
STEAMPUNK

ILLUSTRATED BY BOB BERRY

WRITTEN BY JOEY MARSOCCI & ALLISON DeBlasio

Contents

CHAPTER 1: DISCOVER STEAMPUNK

The word "steampunk" evokes images of dirigibles, unusual characters in sumptuous Victorian attire, and brilliantly modified computers and weapons—all reminiscent of a time that never was. What was previously an underground society celebrated by fantasy-fiction buffs has recently emerged as a pop-culture phenomenon that spans multiple genres. Although the term "steampunk" was coined in the late '80s, the concept of the movement originated in the imaginations of such literary giants as Jules Verne, H. G. Wells, and Mary Shelley, and was further influenced by the scientific theories and ideas of Nikola Tesla, Thomas Edison, Albert Einstein, and others. In the 1970s, these forces emerged as a new science-fiction movement that celebrated the collision of the modern world and the Victorian era.

In this book, you'll be treated to more than a dozen engaging step-by-step projects that will help you develop your steampunk artistic sensibilities. With guidance from the wonderfully talented artist Bob Berry, you'll learn to draw a range of steampunk gadgets, characters, and machines, including a steampunk soldier, a lightning gun, a flying galleon and a pipe organ. You'll learn myriad tips, tricks, and techniques for drawing and adding color, as well as how to use a variety of art tools and materials. Finally, you'll be given a passport to visit—and then to create—a phenomenal steampunk world using acrylic paint as your medium. Throughout your journey, the proprietors of Dr. Grymm Laboratories will provide an insider view into this interesting world, including information about the genre's origins and history, where to gather artistic inspiration, and a brief background about the featured drawing subjects.

Whether you're new to steampunk or you're a longtime fan, this book will give you the inspiration and knowledge you need to create your own amazing masterpieces. All aboard and full steam ahead—your artistic adventure into the world of steampunk begins here!

Steampunk is a popular artistic movement that spans many genres, including fine art, music, performance, fashion, graphic design, and others; however, the inspiration for this steam-driven, industrial utopia filled with Victorian sights, textures, haberdashery, and otherworldly technology was originally born in ink from the masters of science-fiction literature.

Tales of adventure penned by the literary innovators of their time sparked steampunk to life. Mary Shelley's *Frankenstein* (1818) bridged the gap between ancient mythology and the imagination of science, thereby paving the way for the genre's earliest origins. A few years later, the innovative literary techniques in Edgar Allan Poe's horror stories emerged. Then Jules Verne began blending the styles of Poe and Shelley into his cornerstone works, *Journey to the Center of the Earth* (1864) and *20,000 Leagues Under the Sea* (1869). In 1889, Mark Twain pioneered another foundational notion of steampunk with the concept of time travel in *A Connecticut Yankee in King Arthur's Court*.

H. G. Wells is often linked to steampunk most notably for coining the term "time machine" in his work *The Time Machine* (1885), and he continued to perfect the science-fiction genre with *War of the Worlds* (1898). H. P. Lovecraft, a contemporary of the scientific minds associated with steampunk, designed a sophisticated blend of multiple dimensions and apocalyptic settings in a fictional universe known as "Cthulhu Mythos," which he created in 1925. Today, many of these works are taught in high school and college literature courses. In addition to the contributions of these literary figures, the innovations, theories, and ideas of such brilliant minds as Nikola Tesla, Thomas Edison, Albert Einstein, and others also influenced the evolution of steampunk. And many of their ideas thought to be impossible eventually became reality as science took center stage in the late 19th century.

In 1987, science-fiction and horror author K. W. Jeter coined the term "steampunk" to define the works of his peers, authors Tim Powers and James Blaylock. It's likely, however, that Jeter couldn't have foreseen the impact of naming the trend that would later grow into a cultural movement. Today steampunk is most prevalent in the art and role-playing communities. Fans dressed in elaborate costumes and brandishing antiquated-looking props gather at steampunk balls, conventions, and tea parties around the world. And many steampunk artists sketch ideas that they eventually develop into inventions of modified technology, such as operable computers and phones. There are two common principles on which most steampunk artists and inventors tend to agree. The first is that steampunk embodies a "time that never happened." Anachronism does not exist in the fictional world of the artist because technology can develop according to the creator's imagination. The second principle is that the materials used to create costumes, props, and other works of art are at least in part characteristic of the 19th century; therefore, steampunk artists often employ brass, copper, wood, and leather, along with industrial mechanisms, clocks, and assorted machine parts, to create their wondrous inventions. And just as the creators of steampunk envisioned fantastic technological advances beyond the limitations of their era, today's steampunk artists are forever dreaming up new ways to bend reality from a time that never was.

DEFINITION OF STEAMPUNK

CENTRAL TO THE DEFINITION OF STEAMPUNK IS A DISCUSSION OF THE WORDS "STEAM" AND "PUNK." THE WORD "STEAM" IS NOT A LITERAL DESCRIPTION. IN FACT, A LOT OF STEAMPUNK ART DOES NOT EVEN CONTAIN STEAM TECHNOLOGY. RATHER, "STEAM" REFERS TO THE ERA OF STEAM TECHNOLOGY—THE 19TH CENTURY. THE WORD "PUNK" INVOKES THE IDEA OF REBELLION (JUST AS IT DOES IN MUSIC) AGAINST THE MODERN MANUFACTURING AESTHETIC. BUT IT IS UP TO EACH ARTIST TO DETERMINE THE RATIO OF "STEAM" TO "PUNK" IN HIS OR HER WORK.

Steampunk is a burgeoning artistic movement with endless creative possibilities. The key to incorporating the style into your artwork is to understand its roots in the 19th century Industrial Revolution: an era of great change rife with new modes of transportation, scientific discoveries, medicines, weaponry, clothing, and manufacturing techniques—plenty from which to draw artistic inspiration.

When Mary Shelley began writing in the early 1800s, everyday people were beginning to manufacture with steam-powered machines and technology what they previously manufactured by hand in labor-intensive, time-consuming processes. Other innovations of the time included gas-lighting utilities, batteries, and the light bulb, which introduced electricity to the average household. On the communication front, the phonautograph—the first audio recording device—enabled people to send messages via telegram and telephone.

Transportation methods during this time included train, horse and carriage, boat, and even car. Over the course of the Industrial Revolution, roadways, railways, and canals were constructed to transport people and goods more efficiently.

If you found yourself in the midst of a disagreement during this time in history, you would have had several weapons at your disposal to wield against your opponent. If you preferred a blade, you might have used a bayonet, a broad sword, or a cutlass. If you preferred something more sophisticated, you might

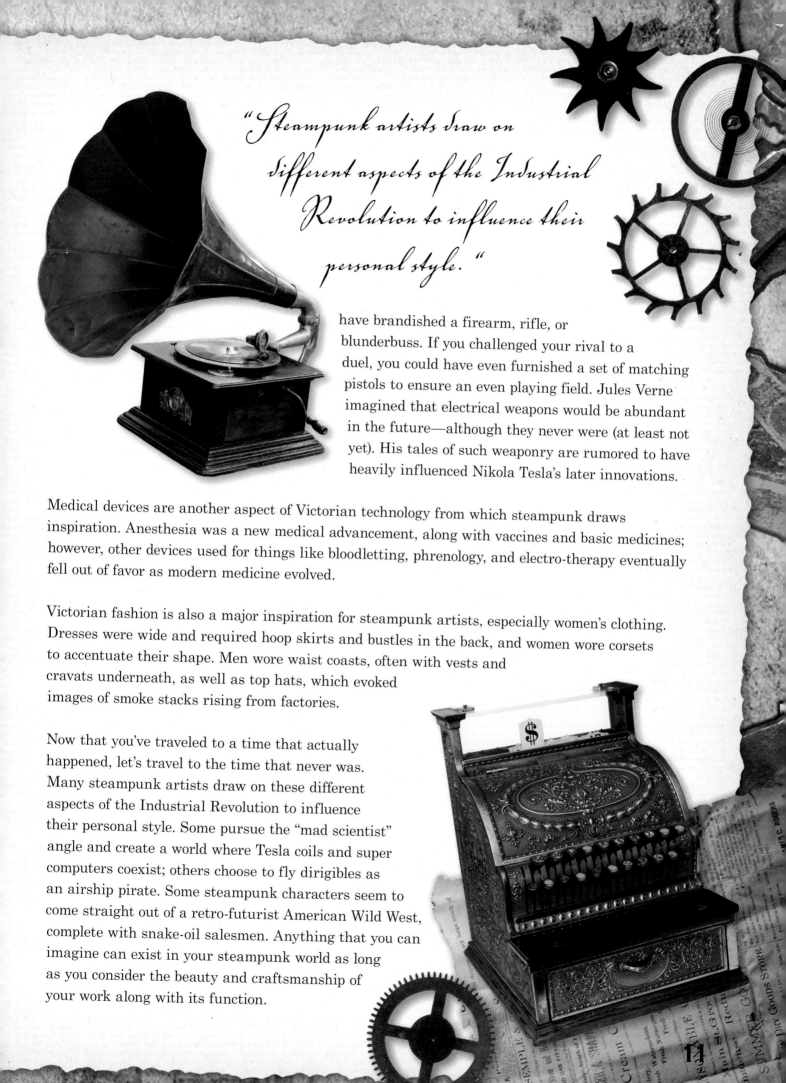

"Steampunk artists draw on different aspects of the Industrial Revolution to influence their personal style."

have brandished a firearm, rifle, or blunderbuss. If you challenged your rival to a duel, you could have even furnished a set of matching pistols to ensure an even playing field. Jules Verne imagined that electrical weapons would be abundant in the future—although they never were (at least not yet). His tales of such weaponry are rumored to have heavily influenced Nikola Tesla's later innovations.

Medical devices are another aspect of Victorian technology from which steampunk draws inspiration. Anesthesia was a new medical advancement, along with vaccines and basic medicines; however, other devices used for things like bloodletting, phrenology, and electro-therapy eventually fell out of favor as modern medicine evolved.

Victorian fashion is also a major inspiration for steampunk artists, especially women's clothing. Dresses were wide and required hoop skirts and bustles in the back, and women wore corsets to accentuate their shape. Men wore waist coats, often with vests and cravats underneath, as well as top hats, which evoked images of smoke stacks rising from factories.

Now that you've traveled to a time that actually happened, let's travel to the time that never was. Many steampunk artists draw on these different aspects of the Industrial Revolution to influence their personal style. Some pursue the "mad scientist" angle and create a world where Tesla coils and super computers coexist; others choose to fly dirigibles as an airship pirate. Some steampunk characters seem to come straight out of a retro-futurist American Wild West, complete with snake-oil salesmen. Anything that you can imagine can exist in your steampunk world as long as you consider the beauty and craftsmanship of your work along with its function.

TOOLS & MATERIALS

On the following pages, you'll learn about the tools and materials you will need to complete the projects in this book.

DRAWING SUPPLIES

SKETCH PADS
Sketch pads come in many shapes and sizes. Although most are not designed for finished artwork, they are necessary for working out your ideas.

PAPER Drawing paper is available in a range of surface textures: smooth grain (plate finish and hot pressed), medium grain (cold pressed), and rough to very rough. Rough paper is ideal when using charcoal; smooth paper is best for watercolor washes. The heavier the paper, the thicker its weight. Thick paper is better for graphite drawing because it can withstand erasing better than thin paper.

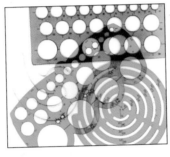

ERASERS There are several types of art erasers. Plastic erasers are useful for removing hard pencil marks and large areas. Kneaded erasers can be molded into different shapes and used to dab an area, gently lifting tone from the paper.

ELLIPSES GUIDE
An ellipses guide provides a useful template for drawing cylindrical volume at varying angles.

COLORED PENCILS
Colored pencils come in wax-based, oil based, and water-soluble versions. Oil-based pencils complement wax pencils nicely. Water-soluble pencils react to water in a manner similar to watercolor. In addition to creating finished art, colored pencils are useful for enhancing small details.

ART MARKERS
Alcohol-based art markers offer a nice finish when applied to photocopies, but make sure that the photocopy toner is dry before applying color. Markers and colored pencils may also be used in combination with paints to further enhance and accent your drawings.

OTHER DRAWING ESSENTIALS
Other tools you may need for drawing include a ruler or T-square for marking the perimeter of your drawing area; artist's tape for attaching your drawing paper to a table or board; pencil sharpeners; blending stumps, or "tortillons," to blend or soften small areas; a utility knife for cutting drawing boards; and an open, well-lighted work station.

DRAWING PENCILS

ARTIST'S PENCILS CONTAIN A GRAPHITE CENTER AND ARE SORTED BY HARDNESS (GRADE) FROM VERY SOFT (9B) TO VERY HARD (9H). A GOOD STARTER SET INCLUDES A 6B, 4B, 2B, HB, B, 2H, 4H, AND 6H. PENCIL GRADE IS NOT STANDARDIZED, SO YOUR FIRST SET SHOULD BE FROM THE SAME BRAND FOR CONSISTENCY.

- VERY HARD: 5H - 9H
- HARD: 3H - 4H
- MEDIUM HARD: H - 2H
- MEDIUM: HB - F
- MEDIUM SOFT: B - 2B
- SOFT: 3B - 4B
- VERY SOFT: 5B - 9B

PAINTING SUPPLIES

SUPPORTS "Supports" refer to the variety of available painting surfaces. Ready-made canvases come in multiple sizes and are either stretched and stapled on a frame or glued over a board. Watercolor and illustration boards work well with acrylic paint, providing a smooth surface. Experiment with different types of supports to see which best suits the needs of your painting style.

ACRYLIC PAINT

Acrylic paint is available in two grades. The highest-quality paints are labeled "artist grade." They contain more pigment and produce truer colors than the less expensive "student grade" paints, which contain more filler. It's a good idea to have two jars of water: one for diluting your paints and one for rinsing your brushes. It's important to keep your acrylic paints moist because they dry quickly. A spray bottle filled with water will help keep the paints on your palette fresh. You can also to keep paint moist by adding acrylic retarder. Do not use more than a 15% solution, as too much retarder can cause uneven drying. There are a variety of acrylic mediums on the market that can help you achieve a range of effects. To create thinner, more translucent washes, you can use a glazing medium or even water. There are also thickening, dispersing, and texturizing mediums available.

BRUSH BASICS

Brushes are grouped by hair type (soft or stiff and natural or synthetic), style (round, flat, or filbert), and size. Whether you choose natural or synthetic will depend on your style and on the investment you wish to make. Synthetic-hair brushes are less expensive, but both types can produce quality work. Among the brush styles, large and medium flats are good for painting washes and filling in large areas. Smaller flats are necessary for detail work; drybrushing; and making clean, sharp edges. Larger rounds and filberts are useful for sketching outlines and general painting, and the smaller sizes are essential for adding intricate details.

Rounds

Flats

Filberts

CARING FOR YOUR BRUSHES

NEVER LET PAINT DRY IN YOUR BRUSHES. WHEN YOU ARE FINISHED PAINTING FOR THE DAY, WASH BRUSHES IN LUKEWARM WATER IF USING ACRYLIC PAINT OR TURPENTINE IF USING OIL. THEN RE-SHAPE THE BRISTLES AND LAY THEM FLAT OR HANG THEM TO DRY. DO NOT STORE BRUSHES BRISTLE-SIDE DOWN.

OTHER PAINTING ESSENTIALS

Other tools you may need for painting include paper towels, lint-free rags, cotton swabs, and a paint palette.

DRAWING TECHNIQUES

By using various hand positions and shading techniques, you can produce a world of different stroke shapes, lengths, widths, and weights in pencil. It's also important to notice your pencil point. The shape of the tip is as essential as the type of lead in the pencil. Experiment with different hand positions and techniques to see what your pencil can do.

WRITING POSITION

This familiar position provides the most control. The accurate, precise lines that result are perfect for rendering fine details and accents. When drawing in this position, place a clean sheet of paper under your hand to prevent smudging.

UNDERHAND POSITION

This position allows for a freer stroke with more arm movement, much like a painting motion. To draw in this position, hold your hand over the pencil and grasp it between the thumb and index finger. Allow your other fingers to rest alongside the pencil. You can create beautiful shading effects from this position.

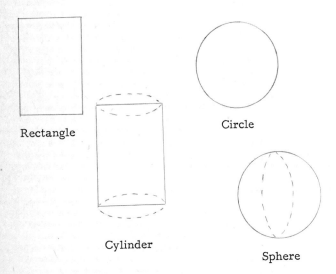

Rectangle

Cylinder

Circle

Sphere

Triangle

Cone

Square

Cube

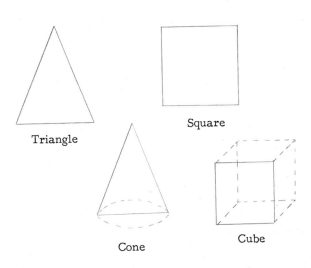

MOVING FROM SHAPE TO FORM

The first step in creating an object is establishing a line drawing or outline to delineate its flat area. This is known as "shape." The four basic shapes, the rectangle, circle, triangle, and square, can appear to be three-dimensional by adding a few carefully placed lines that suggest additional planes. By adding ellipses to the rectangle, circle, and triangle, you give the shapes dimension and begin to produce a form within space. The shapes become a cylinder, a sphere, and a cone. Add a second square above and to the side of the first square, connect them with parallel lines, and you create a cube.

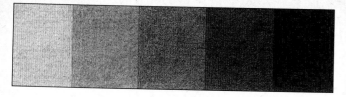

CREATING VALUE SCALES

Artists use scales to measure changes in value and to gauge how dark to make dark values and how light to make highlights. Value scales also serve as a guide for transitioning from lighter to darker shades. Making your own value scale will help familiarize you with the different variations in value. Work from light to dark, adding more and more tone for successively darker values (as shown above left). Then create a blended value scale by using a blending stump to blend each value into its neighboring value from light to dark to create a gradation (as shown above right).

BASIC TECHNIQUES

The basic pencil techniques below can help you learn to render everything from people to machines. Whatever techniques you choose, remember to shade evenly in a back-and-forth motion over the same area, varying the spot where the pencil point changes direction.

HATCHING

This technique consists of a series of parallel strokes. The closer the strokes, the darker the tone will be.

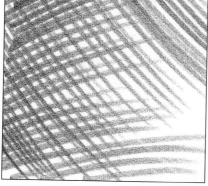

CROSSHATCHING

For darker shading, layer parallel strokes on top of one another at varying angles.

GRADATING

To create gradated values (from dark to light), apply heavy pressure with the side of your pencil, gradually lightening as you go.

SHADING DARKLY

Apply heavy pressure to the pencil to create dark, linear areas of shading.

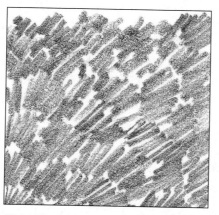

SHADING WITH TEXTURE

For a mottled texture, use the side of the pencil tip to apply small, uneven strokes.

BLENDING

To smooth out the transitions between strokes, gently rub the lines with a blending tool or your finger.

CREATING TEXTURES

LONG HAIR Long hair has a direction and a flow to its texture. Its patterns depend on the weight of the strands and stress points. Long hair gathers into smaller forms. Treat each smaller form as part of the larger form. Remember that each form will be affected by the same global light source.

SCALES Drawn as a series of interlocking stacked plates, scales will become more compressed as they follow forms that recede from the picture plane.

WOOD Rough, unfinished wood is made up of swirling lines. There is a rhythm and direction to the pattern that you need to observe and then feel out in your drawings.

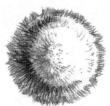

SHORT, FINE HAIR Starting at the point closest to the viewer, the hairs point toward the picture plane and can be indicated as dots. Moving out and into shadowed areas, the marks become longer and more dense.

METAL Polished metal is a mirrored surface and reflects a distorted image of whatever is around it. Metal can range from slightly dull (as shown here) to sharp and mirror-like. The shapes reflected will be abstract with hard edges, and the reflected light will be very bright.

FEATHERS AND LEAVES As with short hair, stiff feathers or leaves are long and a bit thick. The forms closest to the viewer are compressed; those farther away from the viewer are longer.

CLOTH The texture of cloth will depend on the thickness and stiffness of the material. Thinner materials will have more wrinkles that bunch and conform to shapes more perfectly. As wrinkles move around a form and away from the picture plane, they compress and become more dense.

ROPE The series of braided cords that make up rope create a pattern that compresses as it wraps around a surface and moves away from the picture plane.

PERSPECTIVE BASICS

Perspective provides the visual cues that help create the illusion of depth and distance in a drawing. Perspective can be broken down into two major types: linear and atmospheric. In linear perspective, objects appear smaller in scale as they recede from the picture plane. In atmospheric perspective, objects that are farther away have fewer details and appear bluer and cooler in color, whereas objects closer to the viewer are more detailed and warmer in color. With linear perspective, the horizon line (an imaginary horizontal line where receding lines meet) can be the actual horizon or a line at eye level. Having an idea of the viewer's eye level is helpful so you can apply perspective to the forms. When drawing figures, ellipses are especially useful in establishing and enforcing the direction and topography of forms.

FORESHORTENING When the center axis of an object is positioned perpendicular to the picture plane, the forms that make up the object, such as the ellipses in the arm above, appear to overlap and increase in size, meaning that they are foreshortened. Understanding the basic forms and the ellipses that describe the surface will help you understand and draw foreshortened forms.

TWO-POINT PERSPECTIVE

YOU CAN USE TWO-POINT PERSPECTIVE TO GIVE AN OBJECT REALISTIC DIMENSION AND DEPTH. SET UP YOUR DRAWING WITH A HORIZON LINE: A DOMINANT VANISHING POINT ON THE LEFT SIDE OF DRAWING SURFACE AND A SECONDARY VANISHING POINT OUTSIDE THE LINE OF SIGHT, BUT ON THE SAME AXIS AS THE HORIZON LINE. DRAW RADIATING PERSPECTIVE LINES THAT INTERSECT AT THE VANISHING POINT. THESE LINES WILL DEFINE THE PLACEMENT OF VARIOUS ELEMENTS. IN THIS EXAMPLE, THE DOMINANT VANISHING POINT IS ON THE SAME AXIS AS THIS SPEEDSTER'S DIRECTION OF TRAVEL. A DEEP PERSPECTIVE ESTABLISHES A SENSE OF SPEED AND POWER. FOLLOWING THESE SIMPLE GUIDELINES WILL HELP YOU TO CREATE CONVINCING RENDERINGS OF EVERYTHING FROM STEAM-POWERED RACE CARS TO VAST CITYSCAPES.

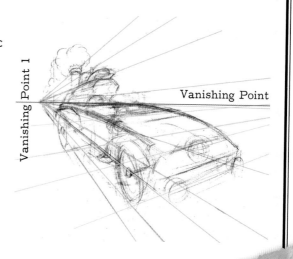

Vanishing Point 1

Vanishing Point

❧ COLOR THEORY ❧

The color wheel demonstrates the relationships among colors. Primary colors—red, yellow, and blue—are the basis for all other colors on the wheel. When two primary colors are combined, they produce a secondary color—green, orange, or purple. When a primary and a secondary color are mixed, they produce a tertiary color, such as blue-green or red-orange. Colors directly opposite of one another on the wheel—like yellow and purple—are "complements." Adjacent groups of color on the color wheel—such as green, blue-green, and blue—are "analogous."

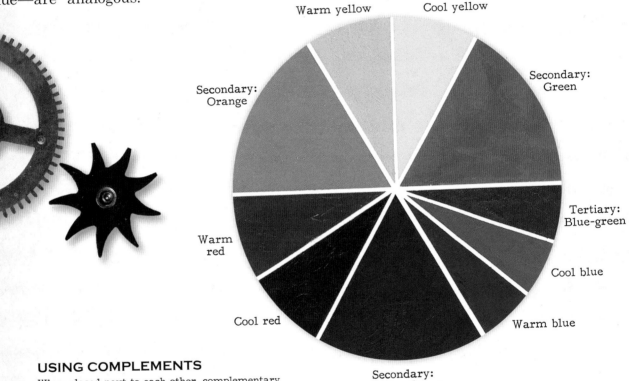

USING COMPLEMENTS

When placed next to each other, complementary colors create lively, exciting contrasts. Using a complementary color in the background will cause your subject to "pop."

Value (the lightness or darkness of a color) and its variations are key to creating the illusion of dimension. You can create different values of color using a basic palette. Adding white to a color results in a tint; adding black to a color produces a shade. The top row represents shading, where black is applied to pure color (yellow). In contrast, the bottom row shows tinting, where white is added to pure color (yellow-green).

MIXING NEUTRALS

Complementary colors make the most natural-looking neutrals when mixed together. Mixing three primary colors will also result in lively, colorful neutrals.

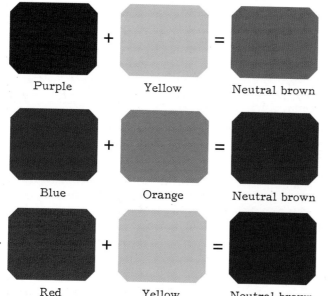

Purple + Yellow = Neutral brown

Blue + Orange = Neutral brown

Blue + Red + Yellow = Neutral brown

CHOOSING YOUR COLORS

THESE 14 COLORS, INCLUDING WHITE, MAKE A GOOD PALETTE FOR BEGINNERS. FROM THEM, YOU CAN MIX JUST ABOUT ANY COLOR YOU LIKE.

Cadmium yellow light

Cadmium orange

Cadmium red medium

Naphthol crimson

Acra violet

Brilliant blue

Phthalo blue

Titanium white

Yellow ochre

Raw sienna

Burnt sienna

Burnt umber

Turquoise green

Phthalo green

COLORED PENCIL TECHNIQUES

Painters mix their colors on a palette before applying them to the canvas. With colored pencil, mixing and blending occur directly on the paper. With layering, you can either build up color or create new hues. To deepen a color, layer more of the same over it; to dull a color, use its complement. You can also blend colors by burnishing with a light pencil or using a colorless blender.

LAYERING
Layer one color directly over the other to blend them together. This can be done with as many colors as you think necessary to achieve the color or value desired. The keys to this technique are to use light pressure, work with a sharp pencil point, and apply each layer smoothly.

BURNISHING WITH A COLORLESS BLENDER
Burnishing is a technique that requires heavy pressure to meld two or more colors together for a shiny, smooth look. Using a colorless blender tends to darken the colors.

BURNISHING LIGHT OVER DARK
You can burnish using light or white pencils. Place the darker color first; if you place a dark color over a lighter color, the dark color will overcome the lighter color, and no real blending will occur.

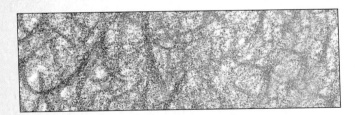

OPTICAL MIXING
In this method, the viewer's eye sees two colors placed next to each other as being blended. Hatch, stipple, or use circular strokes to apply the color, allowing the individual pencil marks to look like tiny pieces of thread. When viewed together, the lines form a tapestry of color that the eye interprets as a solid mass. This is a lively and fresh method of blending that will captivate your audience.

❧ PAINTING TECHNIQUES ☙

The following painting techniques were created using acrylic paint, but you can create similar effects with oil and watercolor.

FLAT WASH
This thin mixture of acrylic paint has been diluted with water (use solvents to dilute oil paint). Lightly sweep overlapping, horizontal strokes across the support.

GRADED WASH
Add more water or solvent and less pigment as you work your way down. Graded washes are great for creating interesting backgrounds.

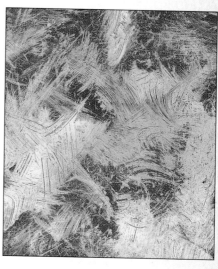

DRYBRUSH
Use a worn flat or fan brush loaded with thick paint, wipe it on a paper towel to remove moisture, and then apply it to the surface using quick, light, irregular strokes.

STIPPLING
For reflections or highlights, use a stiff-bristle brush and hold it very straight, bristle-side down. Then dab on the color quickly, creating a series of small dots.

BLENDING
Lay in the base colors, and lightly stroke the brush back and forth to pull the colors together. Don't overwork the area, as overblending can muddy up the color and erase the contrasts in value.

SCUMBLING
Lightly brush semi-opaque color over dry paint, allowing the underlying colors to show through.

DIGITAL ILLUSTRATION

Digital illustration can result in highly detailed dynamic artwork. Unlike drawing or painting, digital illustration allows you to make dramatic enhancements with just few clicks of a mouse. It helps to have an understanding of the basic tools and functions of image-editing software (this book employs Photoshop®).

COMPUTER SYSTEM

To embark on your journey in digital illustration, you'll need a computer system, a scanner, and image-editing software. In the setup at right, you'll see that you can configure multiple monitors for one computer system. This can help you spread out your work; you can bleed the monitors so that your image crosses over onto multiple screens, allowing you to see much more of the image at once. You can also use the multiple monitors to hold various control panels, so you aren't constantly minimizing windows to create room on the screen. Although it's ideal to work with several monitors, all you really need is one.

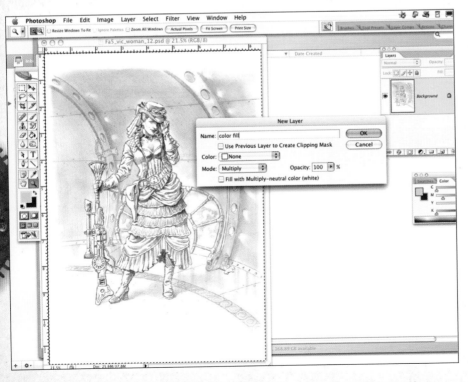

INITIAL SETTINGS

The digital projects in this book use basic Photoshop® settings. First, scan the completed drawing and open the image. Set the "Mode" in the "Image" dropdown menu to "RGB." Set the image to "CMYK" under "Proof Setup" in the "View" dropdown menu. Set the color-mixing palette to CMYK. Create a new layer and name it "color fill." Set the new layer to the "Multiply" mode.

IMAGE-EDITING SOFTWARE

These basic Photoshop functions will help you complete the digital projects in this book.

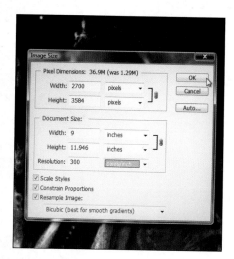

IMAGE RESOLUTION

When scanning your drawing or painting into Photoshop, it's important to scan it at 300 dpi (dots per inch) and 100% the size of the original. A higher dpi carries more pixel information and determines the quality at which your image will print. However, if you intend for the image to be a piece of digital art only, you can set the dpi as low as 72. View the dpi and size under the menu Image > Image Size.

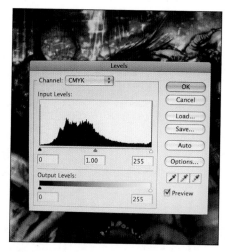

LEVELS

With this tool (under the menu Image > Adjustments), you can change the brightness, contrast, and range of values within an image. The black, midtone, and white of the image are represented by the three markers along the bottom of the graph. Slide these markers horizontally. Moving the black marker right will darken the overall image, moving the white marker left will lighten the overall image, and sliding the midtone marker left or right will bring the midtones darker or lighter, respectively.

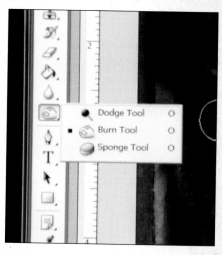

DODGE AND BURN TOOLS

The dodge and burn tools, photography terms borrowed from the old dark room, are also found on the basic tool bar. Dodge is synonymous with lighten; burn is synonymous with darken. On the settings bar under "range," you can select highlights, midtones, or shadows. Select which of the three you'd like to dodge or burn, and the tool will only affect these areas. Adjust the width and exposure (or strength) as desired.

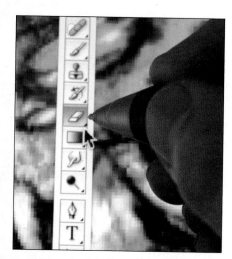

ERASER TOOL

The eraser tool is found in the basic tool bar. When working on a background layer, the tool removes pixels to reveal a white background. You can adjust the diameter and opacity of the brush to control the width and strength of the eraser.

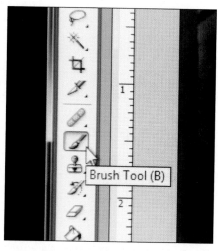

PAINTBRUSH TOOL

The paintbrush tool allows you to apply layers of color to your canvas. Like the eraser, dodge, and burn tools, you can adjust the diameter and opacity of the brush to control the width and strength of your strokes.

COLOR PICKER

Choose the color of your "paint" in the color picker window. Select your hue by clicking within the vertical color bar; then move the circular cursor around the box to change the color's tone.

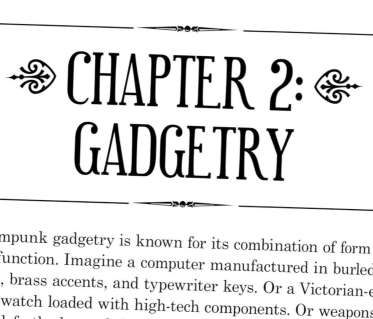

❦ CHAPTER 2: ❦ GADGETRY

Steampunk gadgetry is known for its combination of form and function. Imagine a computer manufactured in burled wood, brass accents, and typewriter keys. Or a Victorian-era wristwatch loaded with high-tech components. Or weapons that defy the laws of physics. With a little imagination, a pencil, and some drawing paper, these are the types of gadgets we invite you to create using the projects in this chapter as inspiration.

❧ SPIDER ❧

With an interior similar to that of a stopwatch and an exterior plated in gold, this tiny metallic spider can sneak up on any target it's programmed to entrap. But while admiring the mechanical beauty of this dark little creature, take care not to become tangled in its web.

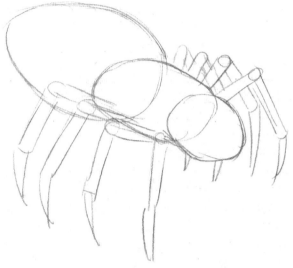

☞ STEP ONE
This drawing closely mimics an arachnid's anatomy. Keeping this in mind, use a 2H pencil to rough in its basic shape; then sketch in eight legs.

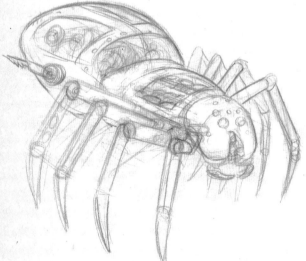

☞ STEP TWO
Draw "windows" that reveal the spider's inner workings. Begin to rough in finely meshed gears and cogs. Note the grappling hooks mounted on the rear of the abdomen. These give the contraption additional spider-like abilities (think "shooting webs").

☞ STEP THREE
Using a 2H pencil, continue to refine the mechanical details. Then add holes to the legs, as well as small pistons. Add pressure valves to the top of the abdomen.

STEP FOUR

Use a softer lead to refine the line work and details. Keep the pencil lead sharp for precise lines and a solid mechanical appearance. Along the legs, draw small rope-like cables, and refine the gears inside the abdomen. Note the addition of the small pistons above the creature's fourth leg on each side. Add more details, such as valves, gauges, and piping to the abdomen. Touch up the shading, and use a kneaded eraser to carefully lift out areas of reflection on the windows. Note the gears that "drive" the spider's mouth mechanisms. Finally, trace over the exterior outlines and windows with a soft B pencil.

☞ **STEP FIVE**

To add a sense of scale, draw in typical Victorian-era workshop elements, such as watch parts, diagrams, a fountain pen and ink, and spectacles.

THIS DRAWING CAN BE DRASTICALLY ALTERED WITH DIGITAL COLOR. FOR MORE ON DIGITAL ENHANCEMENT, SEE "DIGITAL ILLUSTRATION," PAGE 22.

❧ INFOLODEON ❧

The computer mod is a well-known steampunk gadget. Typically, the computer and its related accessories, such as web cams, keyboards, USB drives, and the mouse, are adorned with lavish wood accents, brass antiquities, and rivet-bound leather. These designs start with pencil and paper, but for those with the drive to create and the gigabyte to succeed, designing your own technological system is no more than a click away.

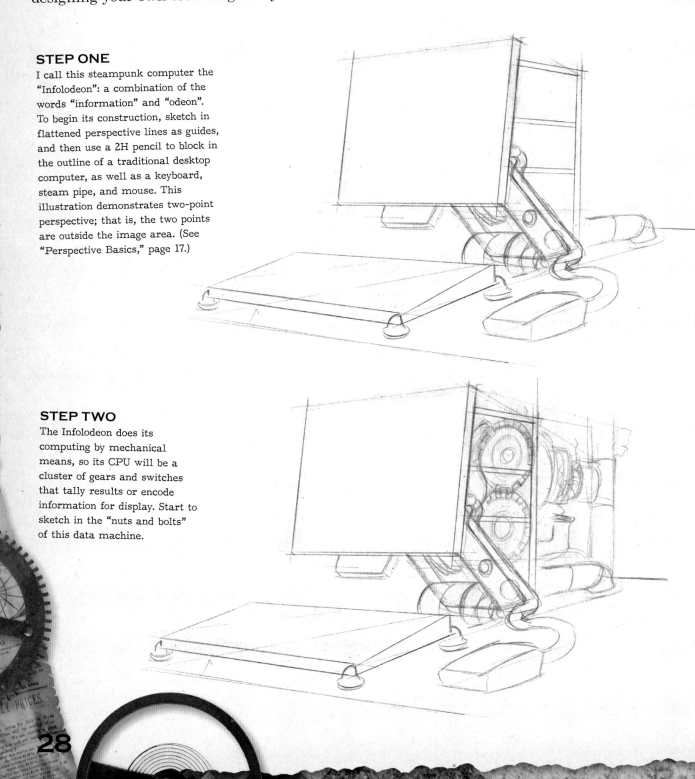

STEP ONE

I call this steampunk computer the "Infolodeon": a combination of the words "information" and "odeon". To begin its construction, sketch in flattened perspective lines as guides, and then use a 2H pencil to block in the outline of a traditional desktop computer, as well as a keyboard, steam pipe, and mouse. This illustration demonstrates two-point perspective; that is, the two points are outside the image area. (See "Perspective Basics," page 17.)

STEP TWO

The Infolodeon does its computing by mechanical means, so its CPU will be a cluster of gears and switches that tally results or encode information for display. Start to sketch in the "nuts and bolts" of this data machine.

STEP THREE

Continue to build up detail using a 2H pencil. Define the gear teeth; then add belts and brackets to the monitor, keyboard buttons, levers, as well as an old-fashioned turnkey to switch the device on and off. When drawing steampunk technology, the more details there are, the better the drawing will be.

STEP FOUR

Begin tightening up the drawing with an HB or 2B pencil. Use a straight edge for the lines, which will also give the machine a solid appearance. Use a kneaded eraser to remove any distracting sketch lines. Note that I've added thicker edges to the keys and the large toggle switches on the monitor.

STEP FIVE

Continue to build up the details. Have fun, and be fanciful with the Infolodeon's design. Add a heavy-duty cable to the mouse and more detail to the monitor.

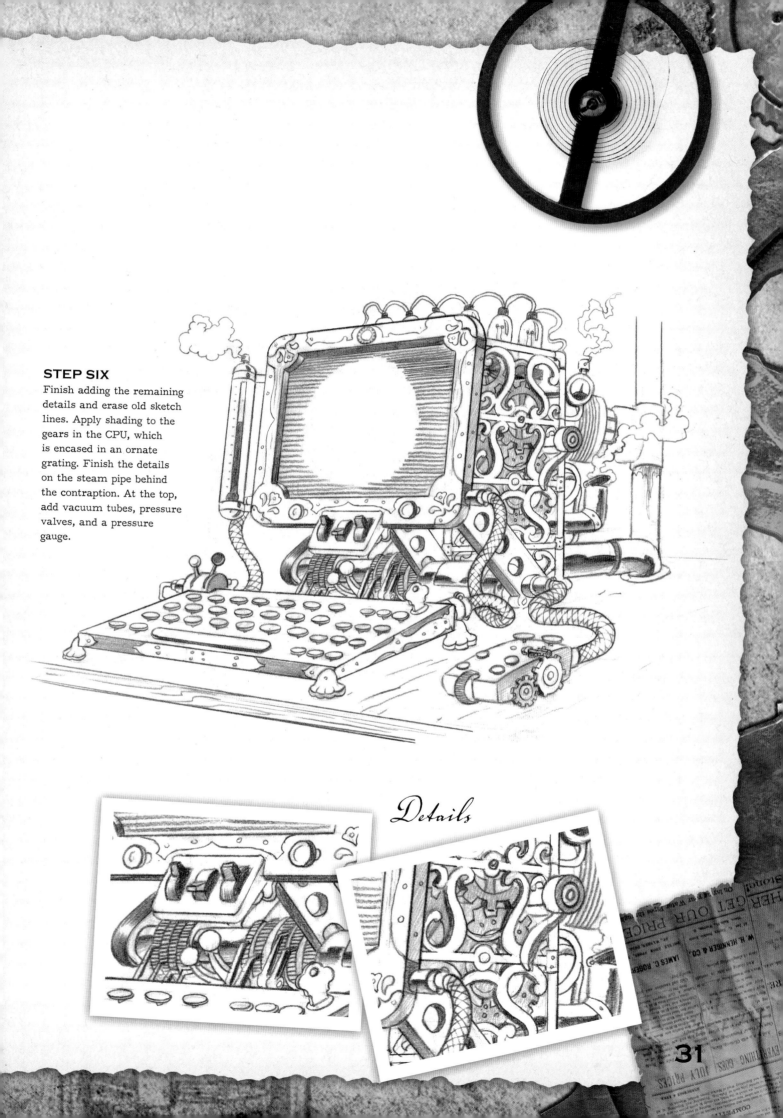

STEP SIX

Finish adding the remaining details and erase old sketch lines. Apply shading to the gears in the CPU, which is encased in an ornate grating. Finish the details on the steam pipe behind the contraption. At the top, add vacuum tubes, pressure valves, and a pressure gauge.

Details

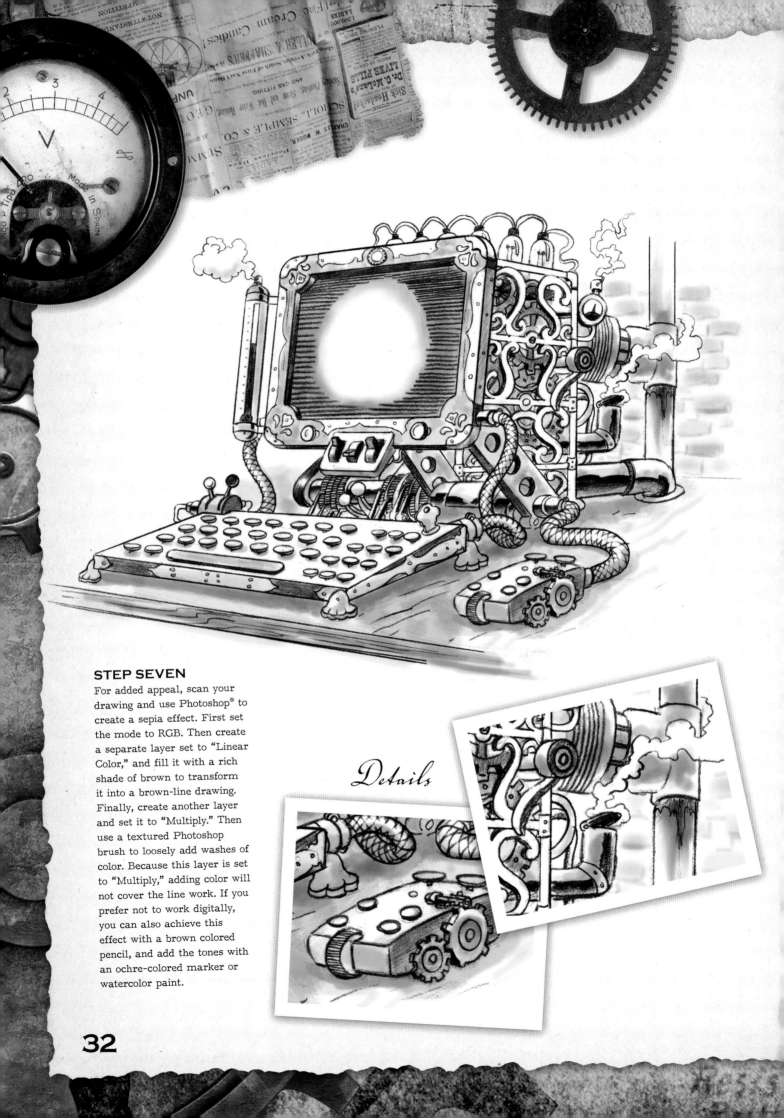

STEP SEVEN

For added appeal, scan your drawing and use Photoshop® to create a sepia effect. First set the mode to RGB. Then create a separate layer set to "Linear Color," and fill it with a rich shade of brown to transform it into a brown-line drawing. Finally, create another layer and set it to "Multiply." Then use a textured Photoshop brush to loosely add washes of color. Because this layer is set to "Multiply," adding color will not cover the line work. If you prefer not to work digitally, you can also achieve this effect with a brown colored pencil, and add the tones with an ochre-colored marker or watercolor paint.

Details

STEAM COMPUTER

WITH THE EMERGENCE OF MODERN STEAMPUNK GADGETRY CAME THE PRE-EMINENCE OF THE MODIFIED COMPUTER. JAKE VON SLATT, ONE OF THE EARLY ARTISTS WHO FIRST MASTERED THIS UNUSUAL FORM, CREATED THE *VICTORIAN ALL IN ONE COMPUTER* PICTURED HERE. HE CONSTRUCTED THIS FULLY OP-ERATIONAL PIECE FROM AN LCD MONITOR AND RECYCLED ITEMS, INCLUDING CURIOSITY SHELVES, A CHINA CABINET, AND BRASS RODS.

☙ LIGHTNING GUN ☙

Ahh...there's nothing like the smell of the ozone as an arc of lighting pierces the night sky and takes down an air kraken (a giant flying squid-like creature). The destructive power of the re-imagined lightning gun reaches back to the stories of Jules Verne, particularly in the novel *20,000 Leagues Under the Sea*—it was Captain Nemo's weapon of choice. Electrical-powered weapons are around today in the form of stun guns and cattle prods, but they don't come close to the imaginary weapons of the steampunk world, such as a lightning gun, which can be rendered to appear dangerous and diabolical.

STEP ONE

This design is based on "Tesla coils," created by the famous inventor Nikola Tesla. Tesla coils consisted of stacked ellipses, which also make up the barrel of the gun. With a 2H pencil, start by drawing several lines radiating from the vanishing point. (See "Perspective Basics," page 17.) Sketch the gun's form lightly, working out the basic angles.

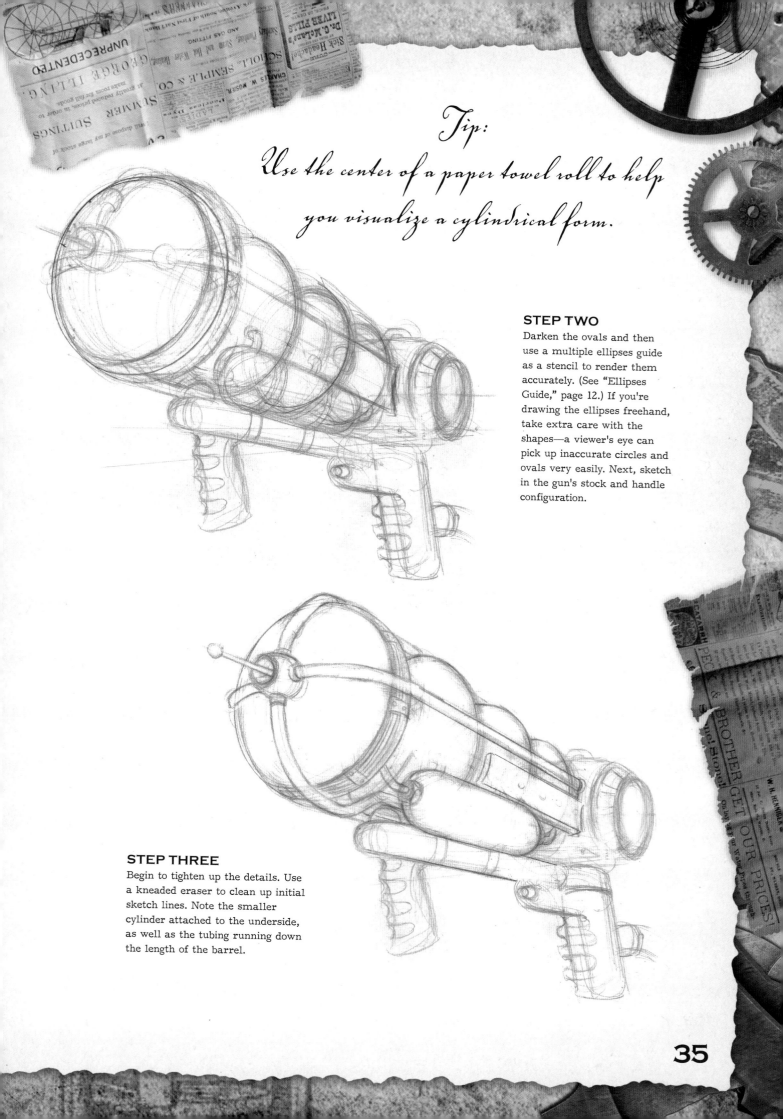

Tip:
Use the center of a paper towel roll to help
you visualize a cylindrical form.

STEP TWO

Darken the ovals and then use a multiple ellipses guide as a stencil to render them accurately. (See "Ellipses Guide," page 12.) If you're drawing the ellipses freehand, take extra care with the shapes—a viewer's eye can pick up inaccurate circles and ovals very easily. Next, sketch in the gun's stock and handle configuration.

STEP THREE

Begin to tighten up the details. Use a kneaded eraser to clean up initial sketch lines. Note the smaller cylinder attached to the underside, as well as the tubing running down the length of the barrel.

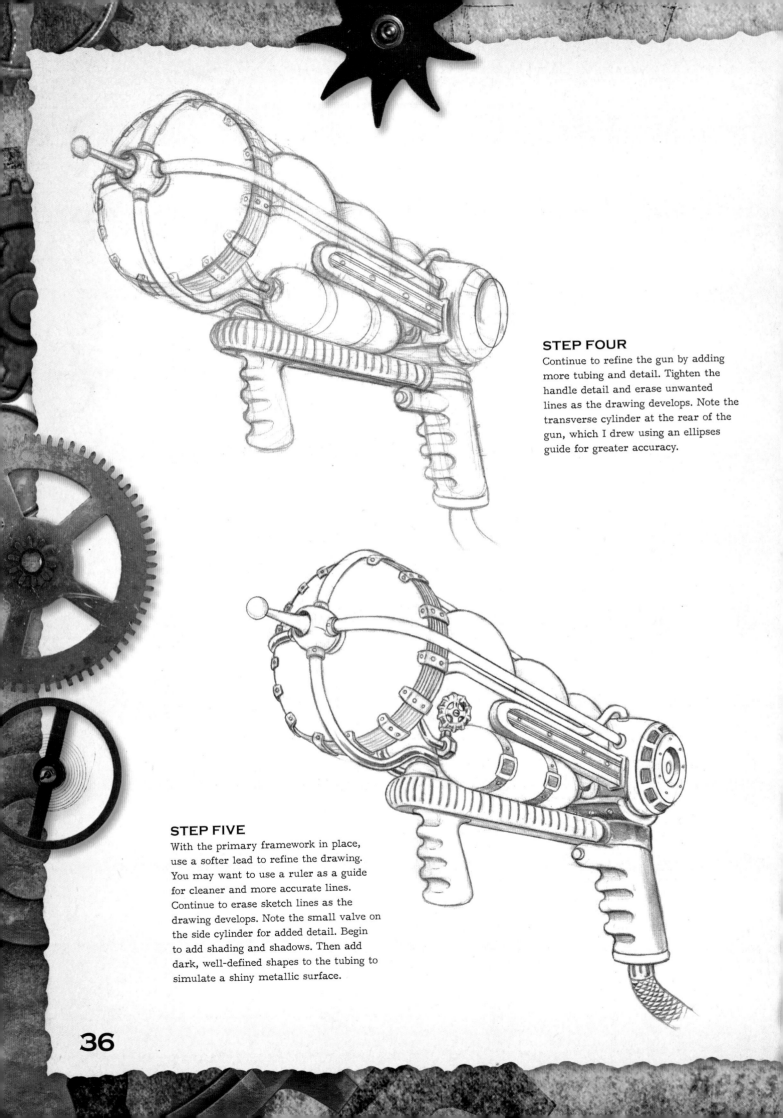

STEP FOUR

Continue to refine the gun by adding more tubing and detail. Tighten the handle detail and erase unwanted lines as the drawing develops. Note the transverse cylinder at the rear of the gun, which I drew using an ellipses guide for greater accuracy.

STEP FIVE

With the primary framework in place, use a softer lead to refine the drawing. You may want to use a ruler as a guide for cleaner and more accurate lines. Continue to erase sketch lines as the drawing develops. Note the small valve on the side cylinder for added detail. Begin to add shading and shadows. Then add dark, well-defined shapes to the tubing to simulate a shiny metallic surface.

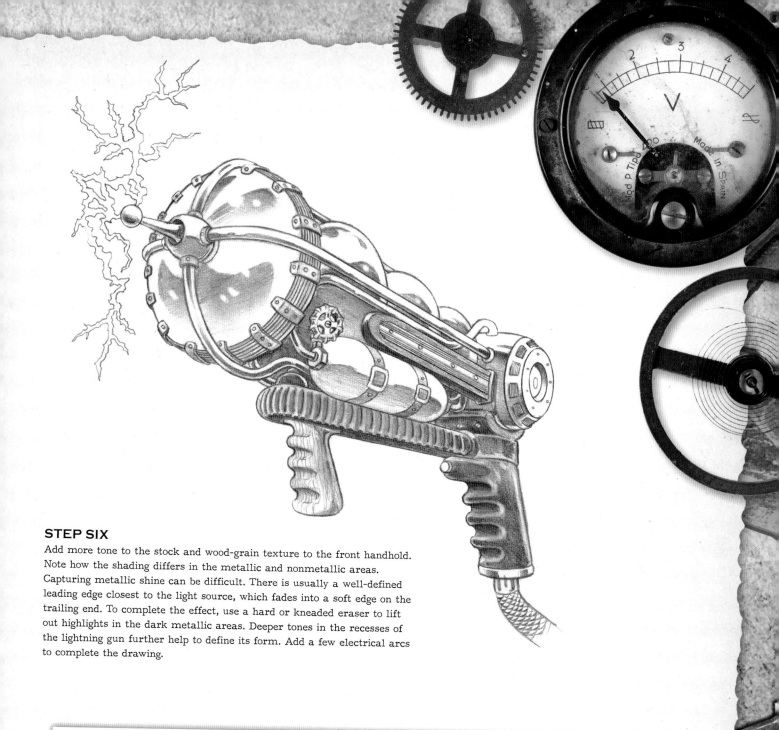

STEP SIX

Add more tone to the stock and wood-grain texture to the front handhold. Note how the shading differs in the metallic and nonmetallic areas. Capturing metallic shine can be difficult. There is usually a well-defined leading edge closest to the light source, which fades into a soft edge on the trailing end. To complete the effect, use a hard or kneaded eraser to lift out highlights in the dark metallic areas. Deeper tones in the recesses of the lightning gun further help to define its form. Add a few electrical arcs to complete the drawing.

THE CLERIC WEAPON

THE CLERIC WEAPON, WHICH WAS CREATED FOR THE HERO IN THE FILM *CLERIC*, IS MOLDED FROM A NERF MAVERICK AND A DOUBLE-BARREL SHOT GUN, AND IT HOLDS SIX CARTRIDGES OF "HARNESSED ELECTRICITY."

⚜ PIPE ORGAN ⚜

In the parlor of the Nautilus (see page 86) sits Captain Nemo's massive yet elegant pipe organ. The droning of the engine and the harsh sounds of steel bending to the pressure of the ocean's depths are joined by the sound of music echoing from the belly of this mechanical beast; however, pipe organs are not just reserved for submarines and underground laboratories. You might find one aboard a dirigible or a steam train. These behemoth instruments of power and beauty produce sound by moving pressurized air through ranks of brass pipes.

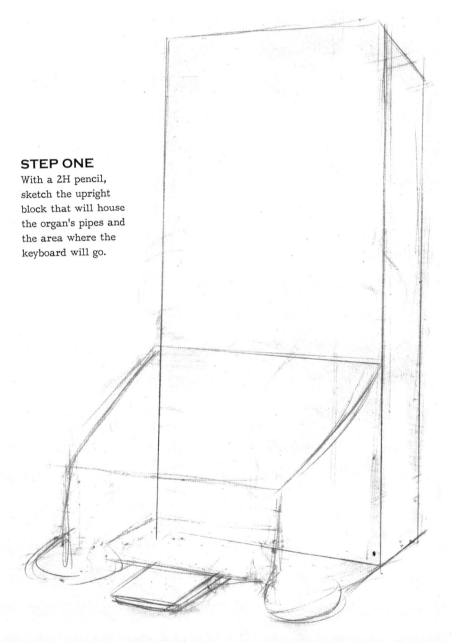

STEP ONE
With a 2H pencil, sketch the upright block that will house the organ's pipes and the area where the keyboard will go.

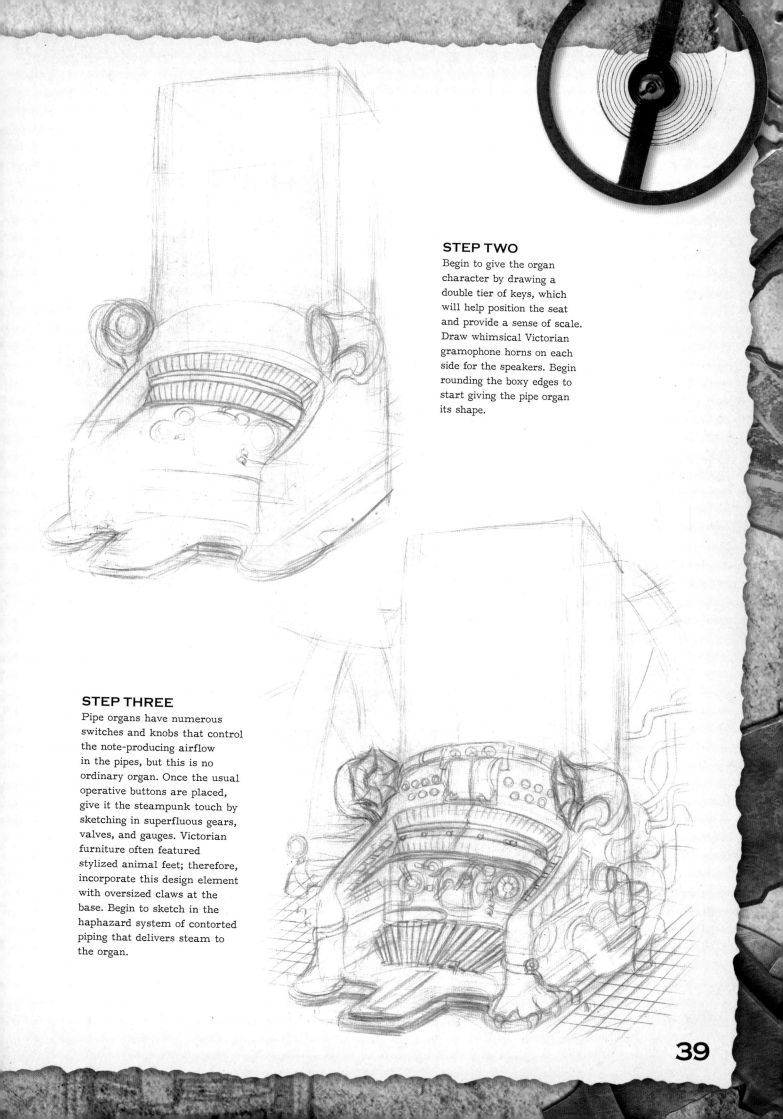

STEP TWO

Begin to give the organ character by drawing a double tier of keys, which will help position the seat and provide a sense of scale. Draw whimsical Victorian gramophone horns on each side for the speakers. Begin rounding the boxy edges to start giving the pipe organ its shape.

STEP THREE

Pipe organs have numerous switches and knobs that control the note-producing airflow in the pipes, but this is no ordinary organ. Once the usual operative buttons are placed, give it the steampunk touch by sketching in superfluous gears, valves, and gauges. Victorian furniture often featured stylized animal feet; therefore, incorporate this design element with oversized claws at the base. Begin to sketch in the haphazard system of contorted piping that delivers steam to the organ.

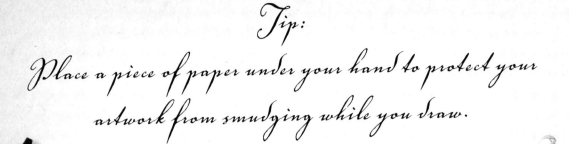

STEP FOUR

Begin sketching in the pipes, varying the layers in size and height. Add the seat, and continue to add and refine the details.

STEP FIVE

Once the sketch is complete, begin outlining the final drawing with a softer B pencil. Protect the fine details of the drawing from your hand with a piece of scrap paper to avoid smudging.

STEP SIX

Use background shading to help define the steam emerging from the pipes. Begin by adding an evenly toned, medium-gray backdrop, softened with a blending stump. Use a kneaded eraser to remove areas of shading to reveal steam. To create the appearance of metal, lightly outline areas of reflected light, keeping the direction of the light source in mind. Then shade around the reflections, making the center of each pipe darkest in value. Lift out highlights with your kneaded eraser when necessary. When adding details to the wooden areas of the organ, such as the legs, remember to follow the direction of the wood's grain and use it to bring out form.

STEP SEVEN
Lightly draw the organ keys. Keeping them uniform may be challenging, but following the pattern of white and black demonstrated above will give them authenticity.

STEP EIGHT

Continue to refine the details, adding gauges and valves below the keyboard and then coating the area with tone so the keyboard appears to recede. Refine the seat to make it appear as if it were made of black tufted leather. Define the remaining components, keeping the direction of the light source in mind.

STEP NINE

Finish drawing the pipes on the left, and use shading to depict form and the illusion of space and volume. Once the remaining portion of the drawing has been refined, lift out highlights throughout with a kneaded eraser. This will create areas of white that further define the organ and give the drawing a rich tonality.

STEAMPUNK INSTRUMENTS

Music and performance make up a significant segment of steampunk culture. Many artists modify instruments to make them appear as if they came straight out of a science-fiction novel. Other artists create new instruments from found objects. But no instrument is complete without a sound system. Some steampunk tinkerers create sound-amplifying components, and some bands even use them to enhance their stage designs. Steampunk fabrication artist Steve Brook modified *The Grand Experiment* guitars with reclaimed gears, gauges, and decorative motifs.

Details

❧ BISON ❧

Most steampunk inventors base their work on industrial inspirations, utilizing materials such as brass, copper, and steel to create weaponry and flying machines; however, there is a unique group of makers who seek to blend the hard edges of mechanics and technology with lines and forms found in nature. These efforts often materialize as sculptures and moving machines that resemble biological creatures, even though they were created from metals and springs. For some artists, mechanical parts alone aren't enough to make their art organic—they marry taxidermy with metalwork, creating a unique style of steampunk art. The bison featured in this drawing project, however, is purely man-made.

STEP ONE
Using a 2H pencil, lightly sketch the basic outline of the bison.

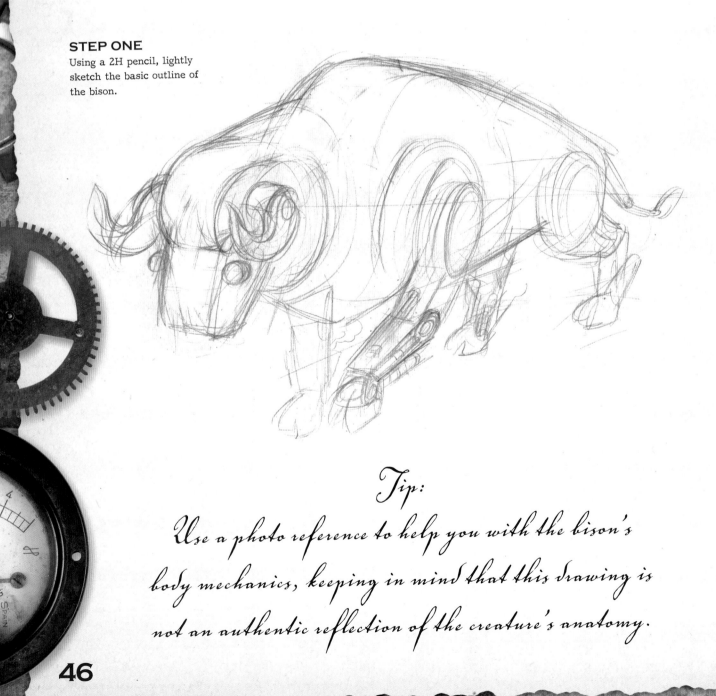

Tip:
Use a photo reference to help you with the bison's body mechanics, keeping in mind that this drawing is not an authentic reflection of the creature's anatomy.

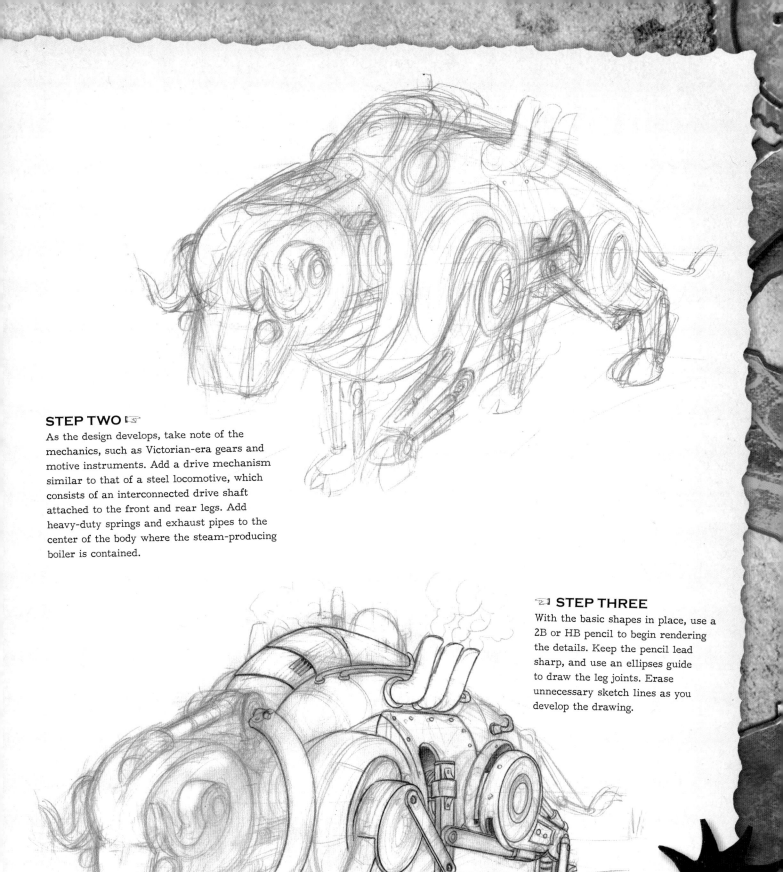

STEP TWO

As the design develops, take note of the mechanics, such as Victorian-era gears and motive instruments. Add a drive mechanism similar to that of a steel locomotive, which consists of an interconnected drive shaft attached to the front and rear legs. Add heavy-duty springs and exhaust pipes to the center of the body where the steam-producing boiler is contained.

STEP THREE

With the basic shapes in place, use a 2B or HB pencil to begin rendering the details. Keep the pencil lead sharp, and use an ellipses guide to draw the leg joints. Erase unnecessary sketch lines as you develop the drawing.

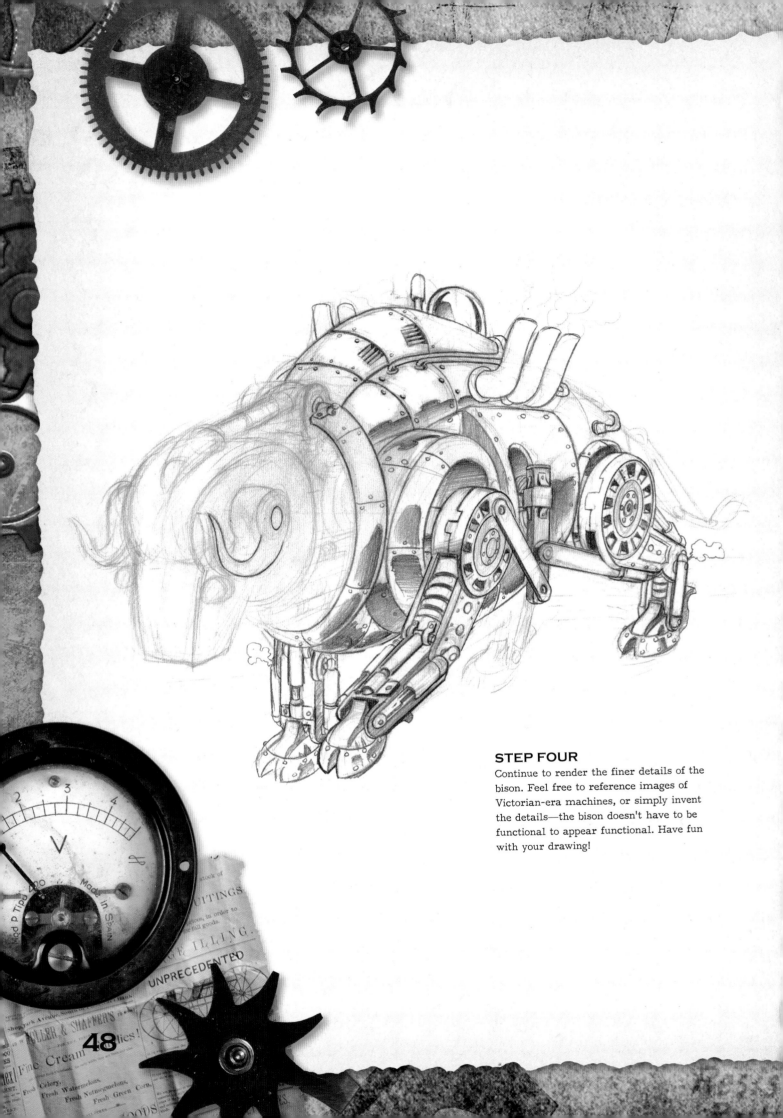

STEP FOUR

Continue to render the finer details of the bison. Feel free to reference images of Victorian-era machines, or simply invent the details—the bison doesn't have to be functional to appear functional. Have fun with your drawing!

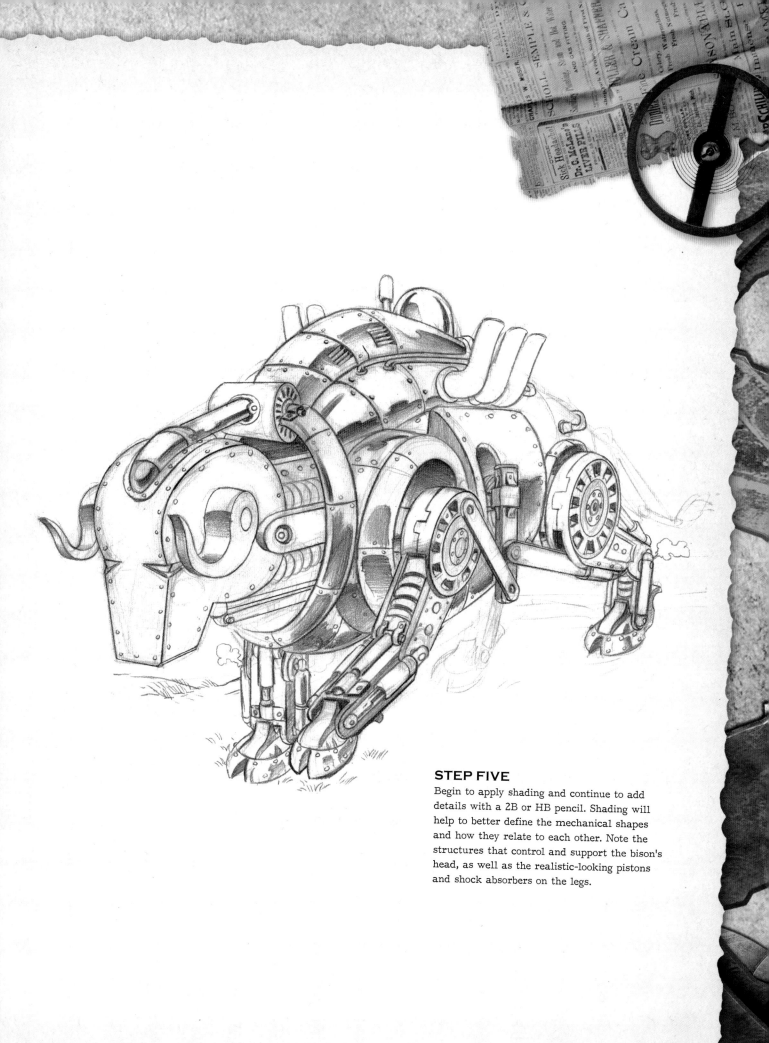

STEP FIVE

Begin to apply shading and continue to add details with a 2B or HB pencil. Shading will help to better define the mechanical shapes and how they relate to each other. Note the structures that control and support the bison's head, as well as the realistic-looking pistons and shock absorbers on the legs.

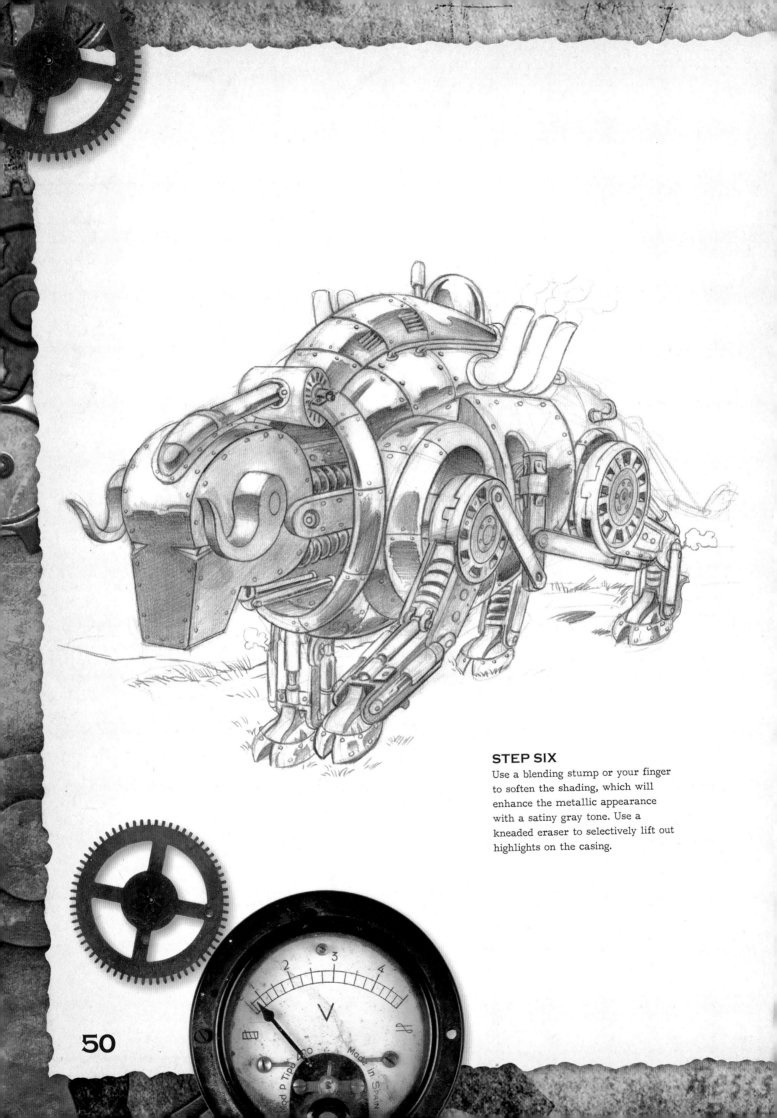

STEP SIX

Use a blending stump or your finger
to soften the shading, which will
enhance the metallic appearance
with a satiny gray tone. Use a
kneaded eraser to selectively lift out
highlights on the casing.

STEP SEVEN

Use hatching and crosshatching strokes to suggest grass beneath the bison's feet. Use the side of a 2B or HB pencil to shade in the smoke streaming from the exhaust pipes. Then use a stump or your finger to lightly smudge the smoke as it trails off into the air. With a kneaded eraser, remove any unwanted sketch lines.

❧ SPEEDSTER ❧

Real-life steam-driven vehicles were developed and manufactured in the United States and Europe during the late 1800s and early 1900s. A steam-powered car even held the land-speed record in 1906 for traveling 127 miles per hour! Meticulously crafted and adorned with brass accents and tufted leather seats, these vehicles transported passengers in style.

STEP ONE
With a brown colored pencil, begin lightly sketching the outline of the speedster within the confines of the established perspective lines. (See "Perspective Basics," page 17.) This speedster borrows design elements from steam-powered locomotives and early automobiles.

STEP TWO
Begin adding the details, referring to the angles of your perspective guidelines and aligning your drawing accordingly. Sketch in a rough outline of the driver, his controls, and the steam engine behind him.

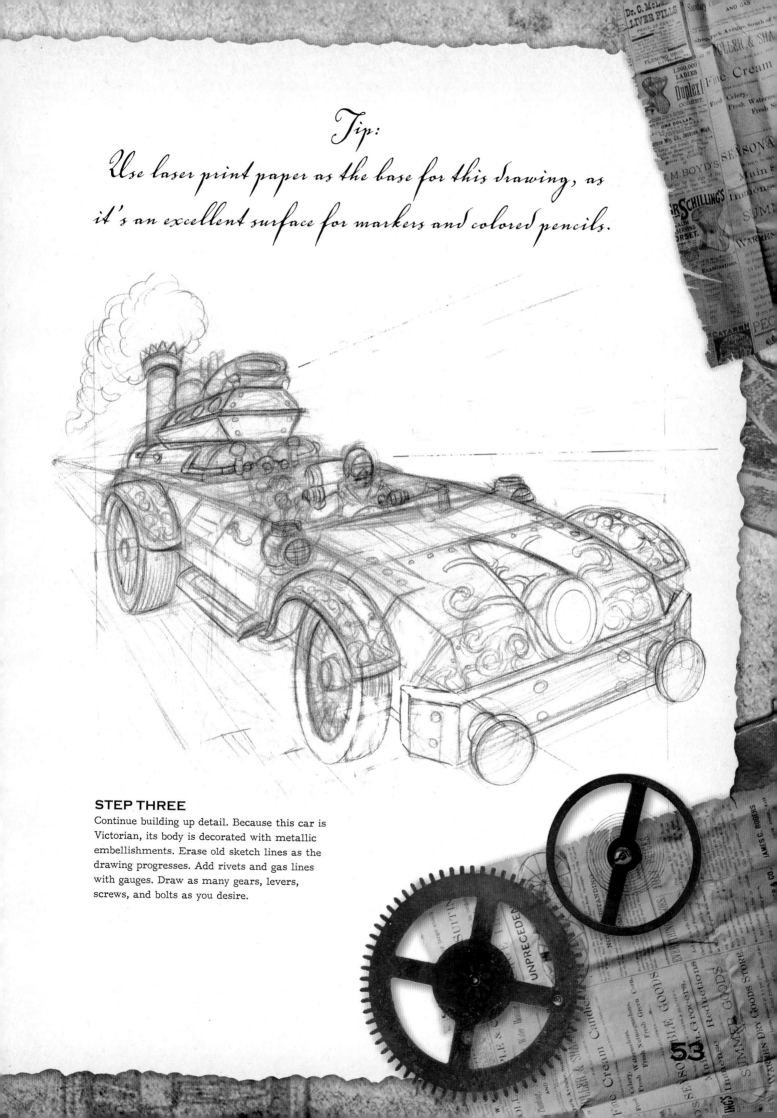

Tip:
Use laser print paper as the base for this drawing, as it's an excellent surface for markers and colored pencils.

STEP THREE

Continue building up detail. Because this car is Victorian, its body is decorated with metallic embellishments. Erase old sketch lines as the drawing progresses. Add rivets and gas lines with gauges. Draw as many gears, levers, screws, and bolts as you desire.

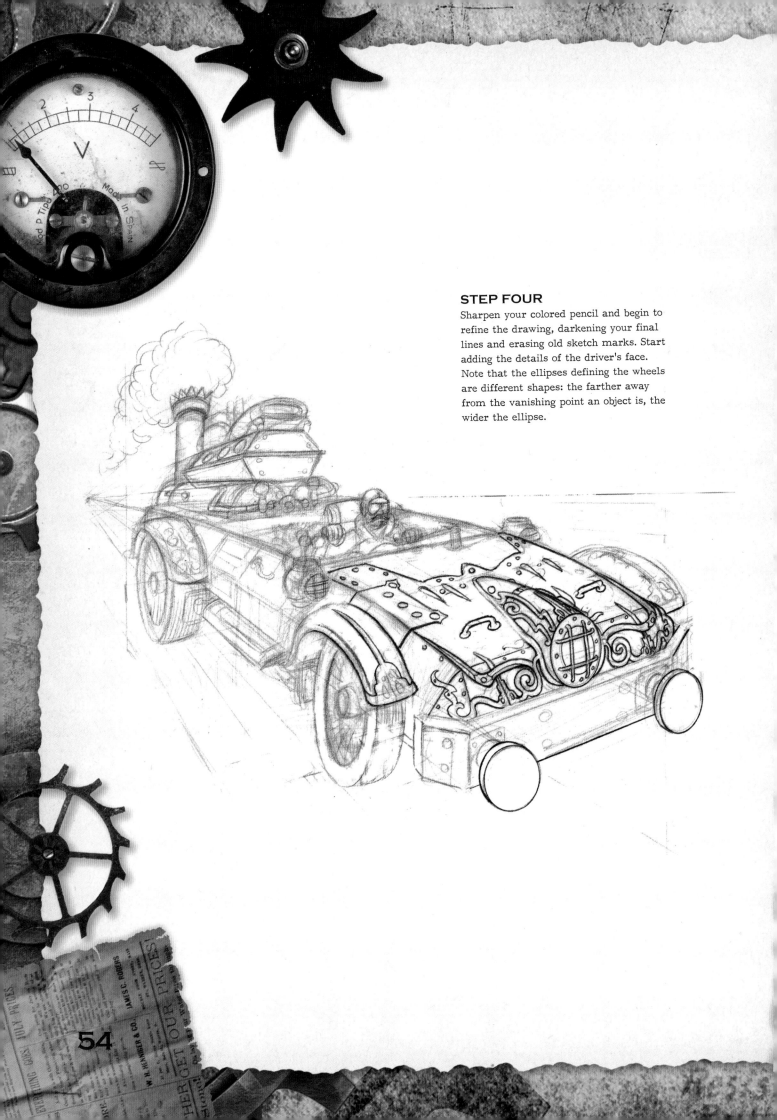

STEP FOUR

Sharpen your colored pencil and begin to refine the drawing, darkening your final lines and erasing old sketch marks. Start adding the details of the driver's face. Note that the ellipses defining the wheels are different shapes: the farther away from the vanishing point an object is, the wider the ellipse.

STEP FIVE

Continue to draw the details of the speedster with a sharp pencil, using shading to represent metallic surfaces. Add the cushioned interior, rivets, wood grain, and other mechanical parts. Take your time refining the driver, the knobs and gauges, and other intricate details that make this subject so interesting.

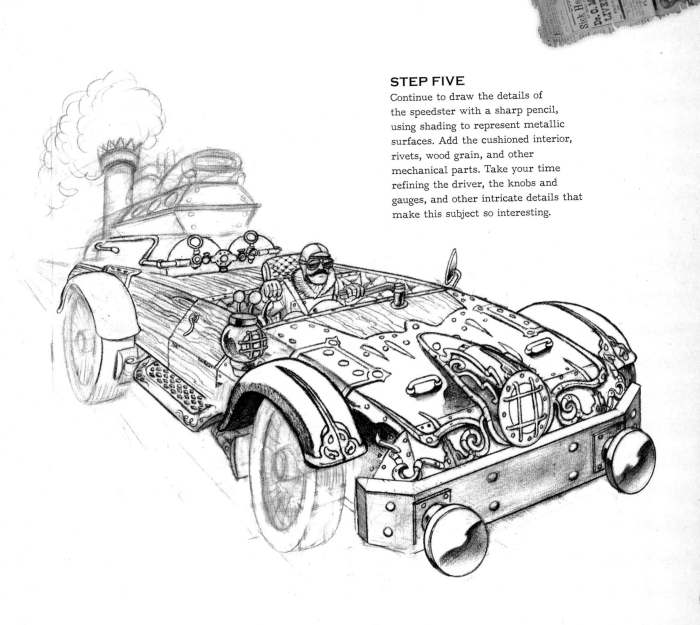

Tip:

Use fine parallel lines drawn in one direction to indicate a wood-grain texture.

STEP SIX

Indicate the spinning motion of the wheels and speed of the vehicle by using feathered strokes that follow the circular contours of the wheels. Draw the large brake pads positioned behind each wheel. Next, outline the motor, fuel tanks, boiler, and air scoop, and then apply light shading.

STEP SEVEN

Complete the smokestack and front wheel, and then clean up any unwanted lines. Finally, add more shading underneath the car.

STEP EIGHT

Filling in a drawing with alcohol-based markers and colored pencils is a quick and easy way to add color with minimal mess. Start by carefully applying color to small areas of the drawing with the thin ends of the markers, beginning with the lightest values. Work in a circular motion to avoid streaking.

STEP NINE

When working with markers, you can apply layer upon layer of color to build up form or to create new colors. Create varying layers and streaks of orange and brown for the wooden panels and fender details. Use a putty-colored marker to create a slight shadow on the speedster's sides and to enhance the wood texture.

STEP TEN

Fill in the fenders with a bright scarlet marker. Then darken the same area with a layer of yellow ochre marker. Continue to add layers until you achieve a rich, red color.

STEP ELEVEN

Render the hood in a brassy, gold color, applying darker colors with markers. Use a dark golden green marker; then use yellow and gold colored pencils to blend in lighter, metallic-looking values. Use the lightest yellow value to indicate reflected light. While lighter areas will be opaque from layer upon layer of pencil, the shadows should be left semi-transparent.

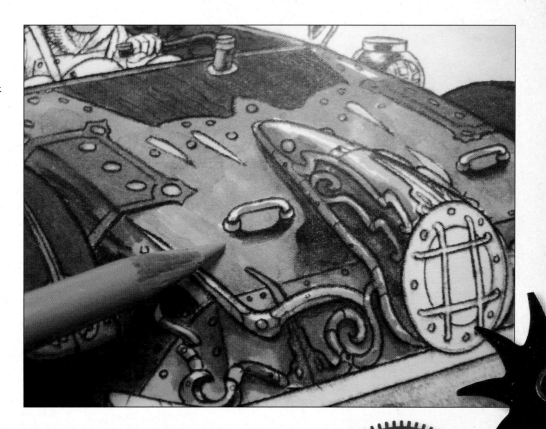

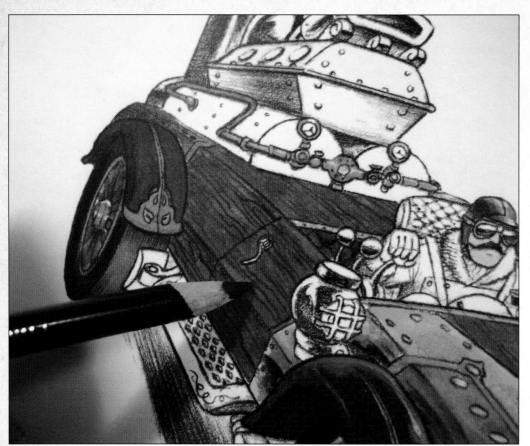

STEP TWELVE

Now use a dark red pencil to create additional texture to the wood areas. I've used the same colored pencil to create the darkest values on the fenders. Use heavy pressure to force the pigment into the paper for a smooth look. A light beige or colorless blender marker can be used to further smooth the dark pencil marks on the fenders.

STEP THIRTEEN

Use light blue and white colored pencils to show light reflecting off the varnished wooden panels in areas around the speedster's interior.

STEP FOURTEEN
Finally, add a little color to the background with markers, and use colored pencils to fill in the ground color beneath the vehicle.

Details

CHAPTER 3: STEAMPUNK CHARACTERS

The steampunk world contains a plethora of characters, including a few archetypes, such as a gentleman and a socialite, who are similar to Victorian-era men and women. If you prefer that your characters are well versed in handling weapons, you may pull a card from an alternate wild west where female gunslingers rule the town. Or perhaps you'd prefer to draw from steampunk's scientific roots and conjure up an inventor building contraptions and scientific devices in his workshop. In this chapter, you will learn how to draw and digitally illustrate many iconic steampunk characters. Then once you've mastered the techniques, you can go on to create your own steampunk denizens.

FIGURE PROPORTIONS

While no self-respecting Victorians would have put themselves in such a compromising position, this disrobed couple will help demonstrate human proportions. First, use the head as a standard of measurement. The male figure is roughly 7 to 7-½ heads tall; the female figure is about 6-½ to 7 heads tall. There are differences in how body mass is distributed in males and females, as well. A simple technique for drawing male and female figures is to use a triangle. As shown in the diagram, the male figure is shaped like an inverted triangle: The shoulders are slightly wider than the hips. The female figure is just the opposite: The hips are wider than the shoulders. In addition to these obvious differences, a female's muscles have less definition than a male's.

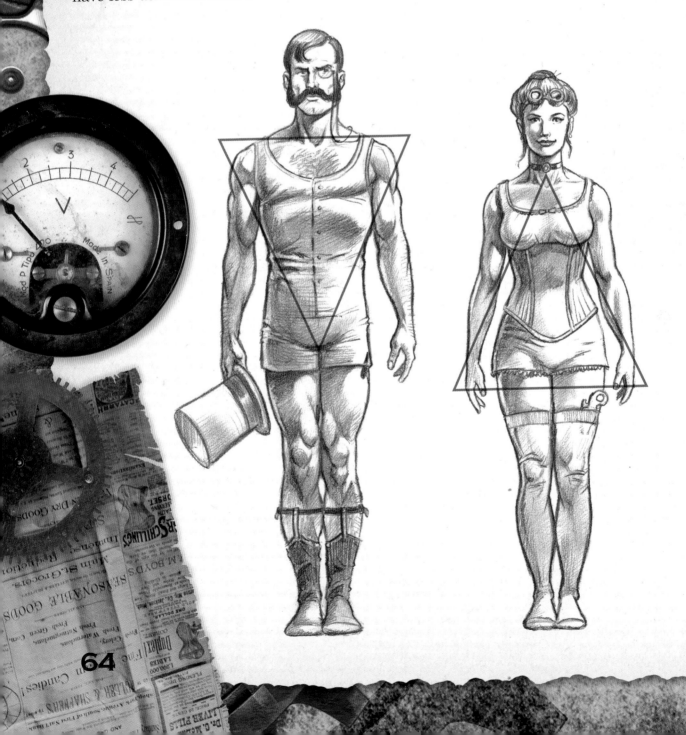

DEFINING CHARACTERS
— THROUGH BODY PROPORTIONS —

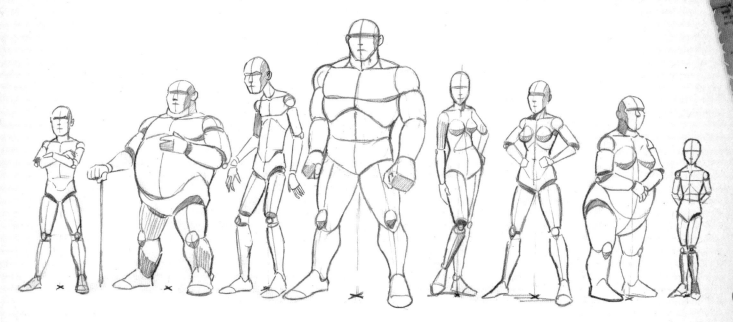

Steampunk stories feature a rich variety of characters. You can establish a character's personality by altering figure proportions, size, and posture. Begin by drawing simple shapes and masses. Once you are satisfied with a character's build, you can begin adding the details.

THE FIGURE IN ACTION

To draw the human figure in action, sketch an artist's mannequin made up of simple cylinders. This provides the framework upon which to add the details.

ICONIC CHARACTERS
AND VICTORIAN STYLE

Costumes are key in identifying the roles of steampunk characters. Apparel can borrow elements from many historical periods, but the classic style stems from Victorian-era fashion. Men typically wear top hats or bowlers, as well as vests, suspenders, and spats. Women have a wider range of styles, from dresses fit for a proper lady to the slightly bawdy, dance-hall inspired costumes worn by female adventurers. Military-inspired ensembles also grace steampunk settings; these usually include campaign tunics, Sam Browne belts, gauntlets, pith helmets, and the ever-present steampunk goggles.

Strongman

Sky Pirate

Gentleman

MALE CHARACTERS
Men in the steampunk universe occupy a wide-range of professions, from blunderbuss-toting gentlemen and innovative scientists to rough-and-ready sky pirates and hulking strongmen. There are soldiers, aviators, and colonial explorers—the possibilities are endless!

Lady

Aviator

Lolita

FEMALE CHARACTERS

Steampunk women are as active and dangerous as their male counterparts, although some, such as the well-armed lady above, have a demure character. The female aviator exudes pride and defiance, and the lolita can be both cute and devious.

❧ SOLDIER ❧

Steampunk soldiers don leather bracers boots and helmets equipped with steam-powered mechanics and weaponry. Goggles originally designed to protect the eyes are transformed into high-powered optics, allowing the soldier to spy on enemies from afar. Survival backpacks are replaced with wearable, pressurized power sources, extendable man-made wings, or jet packs. This solider's uniform borrows elements from the traditional British Royal Guard and World War I gas masks and belts.

✏ STEP ONE
Use a 2H pencil for your initial sketch, building the soldier with simple shapes and masses. To keep the figure in balance, draw a centerline from the top of the head to the bottom of the feet.

✏ STEP TWO
Begin adding the soldier's armor and weaponry, paying attention to the underlying shape of the anatomy.

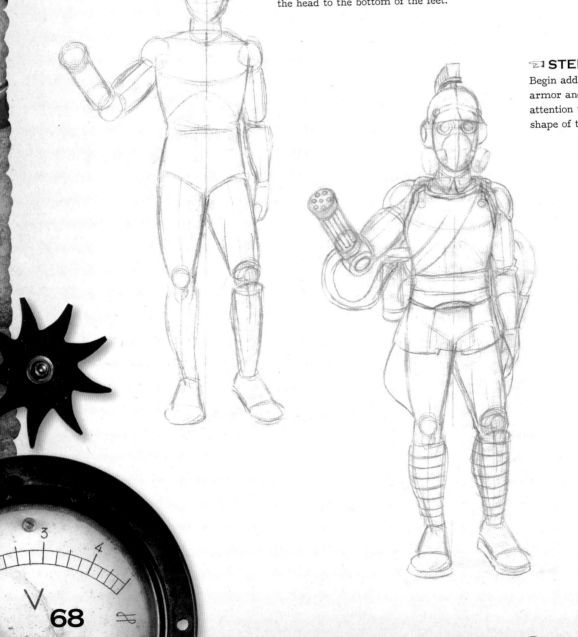

STEP THREE

With a 2H pencil, continue to build up equipment and armor details. Next, tighten the details, including the ammunition belt that feeds into the Gatling gun, the buckles, and the hardware.

STEP FOUR

With a softer 2B pencil, tighten your initial sketch lines. Note how the lines of the soldier's garments follow the curves of his body. Begin adding a soft shadow with a broad, flattened pencil edge shaped with sandpaper. Lightly block in the shadow areas; then fill in the shading. Note how the soldier's slightly raised knee shapes the fabric of the pant leg.

STEP FIVE

Continue to shade and refine the figure's outline, and add a shadow to anchor the soldier in the scene. With the drawing nearly completed, add smoke pluming from his gun, and trace over the lines for better definition. Clean up unwanted lines and refine shading where needed. Once you are finished with your drawing, scan it into Photoshop so that you can begin adding digital color.

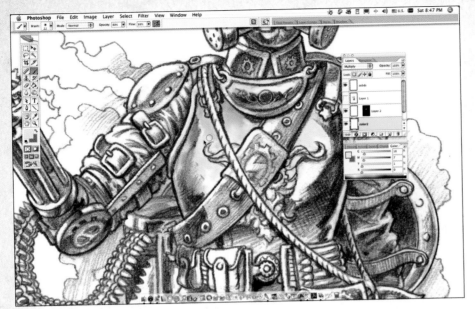

STEP SIX

Create two separate color layers. Set one to "Multiply." This will allow the underlying artwork to show through the color that's applied over it. On top of the main color layer, create another layer set to "Normal." Add touches of opaque color, which will help create realistic-looking metal surfaces.

STEP SEVEN

Use the Brush Tool set to "Watercolor Effect" at 50%. This will give the color application a hand-drawn appearance. Alternate between the color layers to add opaque and transparent areas, slowly building up the color effects.

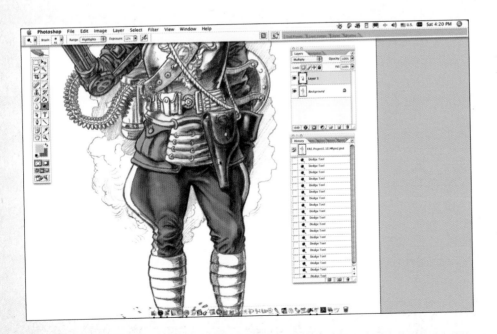

STEP EIGHT

Add slight variations of color to give the soldier's costume a worn look. Use the Dodge and Burn Tools set to "Midtone" to add highlights and shadows to areas such as the soldier's pants. To achieve bright highlights in the details of the soldier's armor, use the Dodge Tool set to "Highlight."

STEAM LADY

Fashionable Victorian-era women were often covered from head to toe, wearing tight corsets and elaborate dresses with bustles and high lace collars. With a few exceptions, they were not expected to develop careers outside of running a household. Instead, these women were raised to be the prim and proper models of respectable Victorian society. The steam lady, however, is a melding of the modern woman and her Victorian ancestors. Her fashion options vary from bustled elaborate skirts paired with tight leather corsets to striped leggings, knee-high boots, and vests fit for adventure. These women happily trade their lace for leather and their parasols for ray guns.

INITIAL DRAWING ☞

Using the tips and techniques described in previous projects, draw a Steam Lady, paying careful attention to the details on her clothing, which are unique to the Victorian era.

STEAMPUNK JEWELRY

MANY ARTISANS TRY THEIR HAND AT CREATING JEWELRY WHEN THEY FIRST DISCOVER THE STEAMPUNK GENRE, CRAFTING WARES FROM DISCARDED POCKET WATCHES, RECYCLED COSTUME JEWELRY, OPERA GLASSES, AND OTHER FOUND OBJECTS TO GIVE MODERN JEWELRY AN OLD-WORLD CHARM. ARTIST AMANDA SCRIVENER CREATED THE *EYE OF THE NAUTILUS OLD POCKET WATCH LACE CHOKER* FROM A VINTAGE POCKET WATCH, A TAXIDERMY GLASS EYE, AND CREAM-COLORED LACEWINGS, SEWN ON A LACE CHOKER ADORNED WITH SWAROVSKI CRYSTALS.

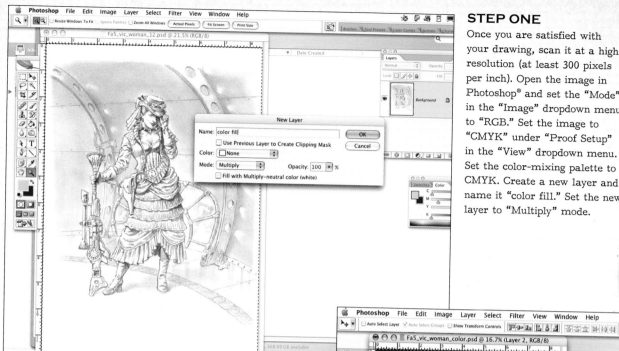

STEP ONE

Once you are satisfied with your drawing, scan it at a high resolution (at least 300 pixels per inch). Open the image in Photoshop® and set the "Mode" in the "Image" dropdown menu to "RGB." Set the image to "CMYK" under "Proof Setup" in the "View" dropdown menu. Set the color-mixing palette to CMYK. Create a new layer and name it "color fill." Set the new layer to "Multiply" mode.

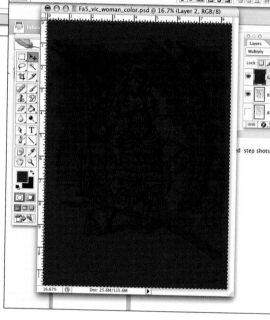

STEP TWO

Use the Rectangular Tool to select the new layer. Then select the "Fill" function from the dropdown "Edit" menu, and fill the selection with a rich, brown color. Most of the painting will be applied to this layer, leaving the original pencil drawing intact.

STEP THREE

On the same layer, add a dark reddish-brown color to the shooting jacket. Use the Dodge Tool set to "Midtones" to begin to build up highlights and shadows on the bodice. Create a subtle, light-ochre skin tone and begin painting the areas receiving the most light. As you paint light areas, the background will define the shadows. Use the Brush Tool on a large, soft setting to build the form of the face.

STEP FOUR

Add magenta lip gloss using the Brush Tool on a small hard-edged setting. Continue to use a light, muted tan to build the woman's features. With the Dodge Tool, carefully create a high area of light on the cheek. Then create a highlight in the hair to give the illusion of hair color. Use 20% black to paint in the white of the eyes. Turn down the opacity of the brush to 50% to slowly build the strongest value of light gray. Continue to apply the Dodge Tool to the woman's tresses, and use a tapering brush to apply additional natural-looking highlights to the hair.

STEP FIVE

Using the Brush Tool, apply a dark, warm gray to the gloves. Once they're filled in, use the Dodge Tool to bring out highlights, switching back and forth between "Midtone" and "Highlight" mode for the best results. Use the highlight setting last and sparingly.

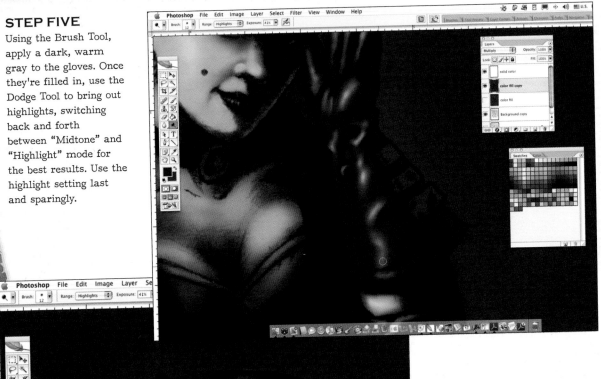

STEP SIX

Paint the hat with a dark green that edges on black. Use the magic wand (Quick Selection Tool) to select the painted area of the hat to isolate it from the background. Then use the Dodge Tool at a low setting to bring out a green-hued highlight on the top plane. Reset the Dodge Tool to "Midtone," and apply to the side of the hat for a slightly darker, cooler highlight. The changing color modulations help define the changing planes of the hat. Use the Dodge Tool to bring out the brass color on the goggles and the satin rim of the hat.

STEP SEVEN

Use the Dodge Tool to apply a light golden-yellow highlight on the buttons. Next, use the "Edit in Quick Mask Mode" Tool to apply a mask to the window, which will allow you to color the scene through the window without affecting painted areas. Set the mask to any color you prefer.

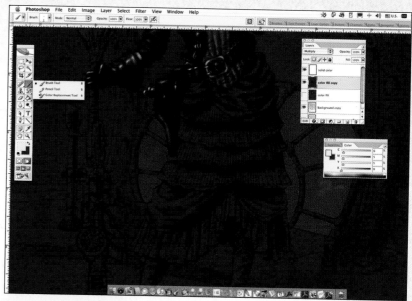

STEP EIGHT

Use the "Load Selection" function to turn your mask into an active selection. Save this selection, as you may need to use it again. With the interior of the windows selected, activate Hue/Saturation in the "Image" dropdown menu under "Adjustments" to brighten and de-saturate color in the windows to gray. With the selection still active, use the Dodge and Burn Tools to render clouds. Invert the selected area and use the Dodge Tool to add a brass tonality to the window framework.

STEP NINE

Use the Quick Mask Tool to mask off the skirt. Activate the mask and use the Burn Tool to fill in the selection with dark green. Use the Burn Tool set to "Midtone" to add even darker shadows to this area. Switch to the Dodge Tool and begin to add shiny highlights to the skirt trim. Follow-up with the Dodge Tool on a broad setting to add pleat and fold highlights to the skirt.

STEP TEN

Use the Dodge Tool to add shine to the floor showing where reflected light passes through the window. Then color the bodice in a shade similar to the gloves. Apply brown to the wooden portions of the blunderbuss, and then use a golden-yellow and lighter gunmetal color for the remaining sections. Add a red stripe to the edge of the carpeting, and add texture and color modulation with the Brush Tool set to a textured mark. Finally, paint the ribbon attached to the bonnet in red with the Brush Tool set to 85% opacity. Build up form by painting increasingly opaque values of red.

STEAMPUNK IN THE MOVIES

STEAMPUNK-STYLE ART, PROPS, AND CHARACTERS HAVE APPEARED IN MOVIES SINCE CINEMA'S INCEPTION. THOUGH MANY FILMS CAN BE CONSIDERED STEAMPUNK, THERE IS NOT A QUINTESSENTIAL FILM THAT SERVES AS A PURE EXAMPLE OF THE GENRE. IN 1902, GEORGES MÉLIÈS DIRECTED AND STARRED IN ONE OF THE EARLIEST STEAMPUNK-THEMED FILMS TITLED, *A TRIP TO THE MOON*. THIS SCIENCE-FICTION-BASED SILENT MOVIE EMPLOYED GROUND-BREAKING SETS AND SPECIAL EFFECTS FOR THE TIME. OTHER FILMS WORTH NOTING FOR THEIR ACHIEVEMENT, INNOVATION, AND IMPLEMENTATION OF SPECIAL EFFECTS AND DESIGN ARE *20,000 LEAGUES UNDER THE SEA* (1954) AND *THE TIME MACHINE* (1960). AND NO DISCUSSION OF CLASSIC SCIENCE-FICTION CINEMA WOULD BE COMPLETE WITHOUT MENTIONING *FRANKENSTEIN* (1931). AS ONE OF THE ORIGINAL LITERARY REFERENCES FOR STEAMPUNK, IT SEEMS FITTING THAT THIS MOVIE WOULD CONTINUE TO INSPIRE MAD SCIENTISTS EVEN TODAY.

DR. GRYMM'S TOP 10 STEAMPUNK-RELATED MOVIES

· *20,000 LEAGUES UNDER THE SEA* (1954)

· *THE TIME MACHINE* (1960)

· *BRAZIL* (1985)

· *BACK TO THE FUTURE III* (1990)

· *THE CITY OF LOST CHILDREN* (1995)

· *WILD WILD WEST* (1999)

· *THE LEAGUE OF EXTRAORDINARY GENTLEMEN* (2003)

· *STEAMBOY* (2004)

· *HELLBOY II: THE GOLDEN ARMY* (2008)

· *9* (2009)

❧ VILLAIN ❧

Lounging in a parlor, wearing an elegant silk smoking jacket, and discussing his latest conquest is routine for the dashing Victorian villain. A Victorian gentleman's endeavors often revolved around winning the heart of a beautiful young woman or adding a piece of land to the family plot. The conquests of the steampunk villain are far more sinister. He may attempt world domination armed with death rays or a robotic army, or he may wish to alter history using time travel. His minions build his mechanical inventions, which are designed to destroy the world, but the steampunk villain always assumes the accolades for these "accomplishments."

INITIAL DRAWING ☞

Using the tips and techniques described in previous projects, draw a Villain, paying attention to the clothing details, which are unique to the Victorian era.

STEP ONE

Scan the completed drawing at a high-resolution (at least 300 pixels per inch). Open the image in Photoshop and set the "Mode" in the "Image" dropdown menu to "RGB." Set the image to "CMYK" under "Proof Setup" in the "View" dropdown menu. Set the color-mixing palette to CMYK. Create a new layer and name it "color fill." Set the new layer to the "Multiply" mode.

STEP TWO

Use the Rectangular Tool to select the new layer. Then select the "Fill" function from the dropdown "Edit" menu and fill the selection with a rich, brown color. Most of the painting will be applied to this layer, leaving the original pencil drawing intact.

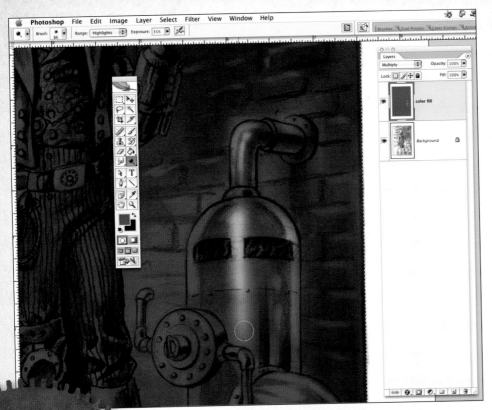

▣ **STEP THREE**

To create the majority of the detail in this project, use the Dodge and Burn Tools to modulate the brown color superimposed over the entire image. Use the Dodge Tool with the "Range" set to "Midtones" to add highlights to the metal pipes and cylinder. Next, reset the Dodge Tool's "Range" to "Highlights" and go over areas you've already lightened to create brassy highlights.

STEP FOUR ☞

Now select the Brush Tool, create a dark gray-brown in the color palette, and then paint the jacket. Next, use the Burn Tool to add some heavy shading, and use the Dodge Tool to create highlights where the lamplight illuminates the villain. When satisfied with the appearance of the jacket, add dark gray to the vest and trousers.

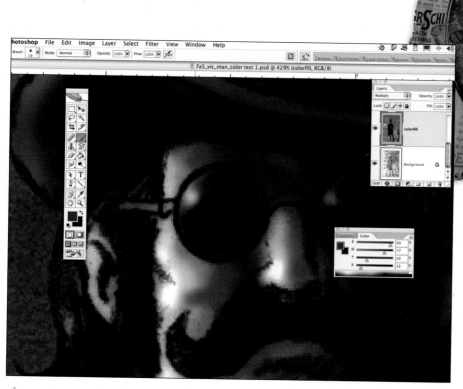

☞ STEP FIVE

Now zoom in on the face. Paint the side of the face with a warm beige to bring out the facial planes that catch light. Next, use the Blur Tool to soften the harder edges of the painted areas, and use the Burn and Dodge Tools to add shadow to the face. Paint the lenses of the glasses dark blue and then lighten them around the edges. The highlights on the lenses are cyan lightened with the Dodge Tool's "Range" set to "Highlights." Add warm highlights on the face using the Dodge Tool at the same setting.

☞ STEP SIX

Use the Dodge Tool to create a halo around the street lamp with subtle rays emanating outward. Switch to the Brush Tool and paint an area of light, warm yellow inside the lamp, and highlight the center with the Dodge Tool's "Range" set to "Highlight." Mix a dark, warm gray, and with the Brush Tool set to a 60% fade (in the brush palette), darken parts of the metalwork on the lamp. Paint the heaviest values at the top of the lamp; then fade the color into the fog.

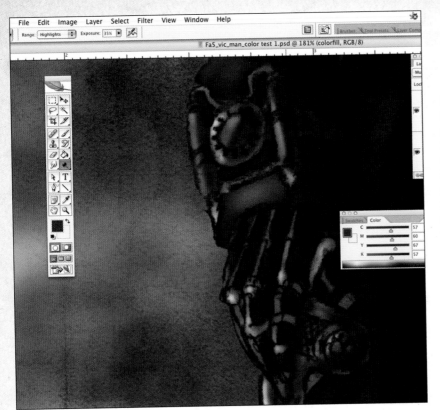

STEP SEVEN

Zoom in on the hardware adorning the villain's hands. Use the Dodge Tool to create light brassy tones in the background. Work the area several times, creating the highlights in stages. Next, mix a golden yellow color to enhance the brassy tones. Then use the Dodge Tool to further enhance the highlights. Repeat this process on the other arm.

THE WHOLE 9 YARDS GOGGLES BY DR. GRYMM FEATURE REMOVABLE FOLDING SCISSORS, PINCUSHIONS, INTERCHANGEABLE THREAD BOBBINS, AND MAGNIFIERS. SEVERAL VERSIONS OF THIS ORIGINAL PAIR OF GOGGLES HAVE BEEN CREATED FOR PRIVATE COLLECTORS AROUND THE WORLD.

STEP EIGHT

Continue using techniques from previous steps to build the image. Add solid highlights in various places on the third layer, and use the Dodge Tool to further enhance the fog. Apply blue to the ground and then streak it with the Dodge Tool to simulate wet pavement. Finally, use a soft brush loaded with yellow to spray glowing effects on the third layer.

83

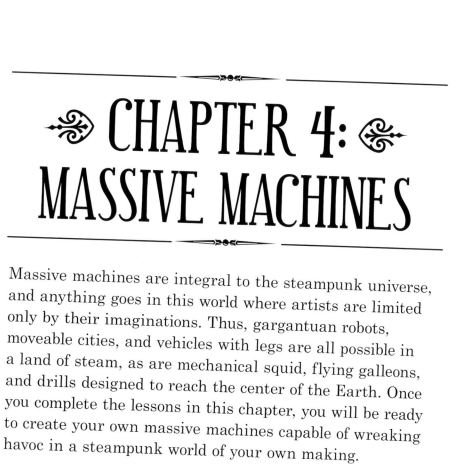

❧ CHAPTER 4: ❧
MASSIVE MACHINES

Massive machines are integral to the steampunk universe, and anything goes in this world where artists are limited only by their imaginations. Thus, gargantuan robots, moveable cities, and vehicles with legs are all possible in a land of steam, as are mechanical squid, flying galleons, and drills designed to reach the center of the Earth. Once you complete the lessons in this chapter, you will be ready to create your own massive machines capable of wreaking havoc in a steampunk world of your own making.

❧ NAUTILUS ❧

The Nautilus has had many incarnations through the years. The most famous is Captain Nemo's vessel in Jules Verne's literary classic, *20,000 Leagues Under the Sea*. With all the power of a war machine and all the comforts of a Victorian home, the Nautilus contains a parlor, library, dining area, and even a pipe organ—all hidden beneath the ocean's depths. This legendary ship will inspire artists and engineers for years to come.

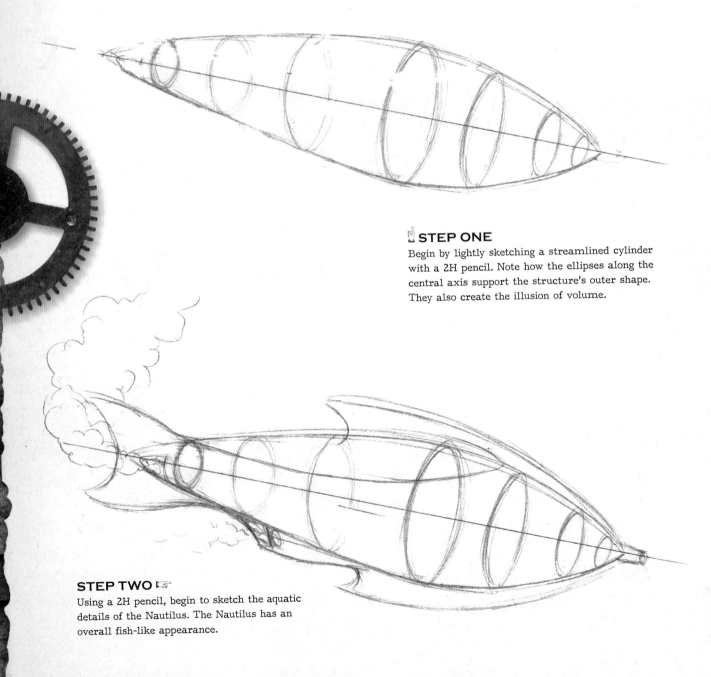

STEP ONE
Begin by lightly sketching a streamlined cylinder with a 2H pencil. Note how the ellipses along the central axis support the structure's outer shape. They also create the illusion of volume.

STEP TWO
Using a 2H pencil, begin to sketch the aquatic details of the Nautilus. The Nautilus has an overall fish-like appearance.

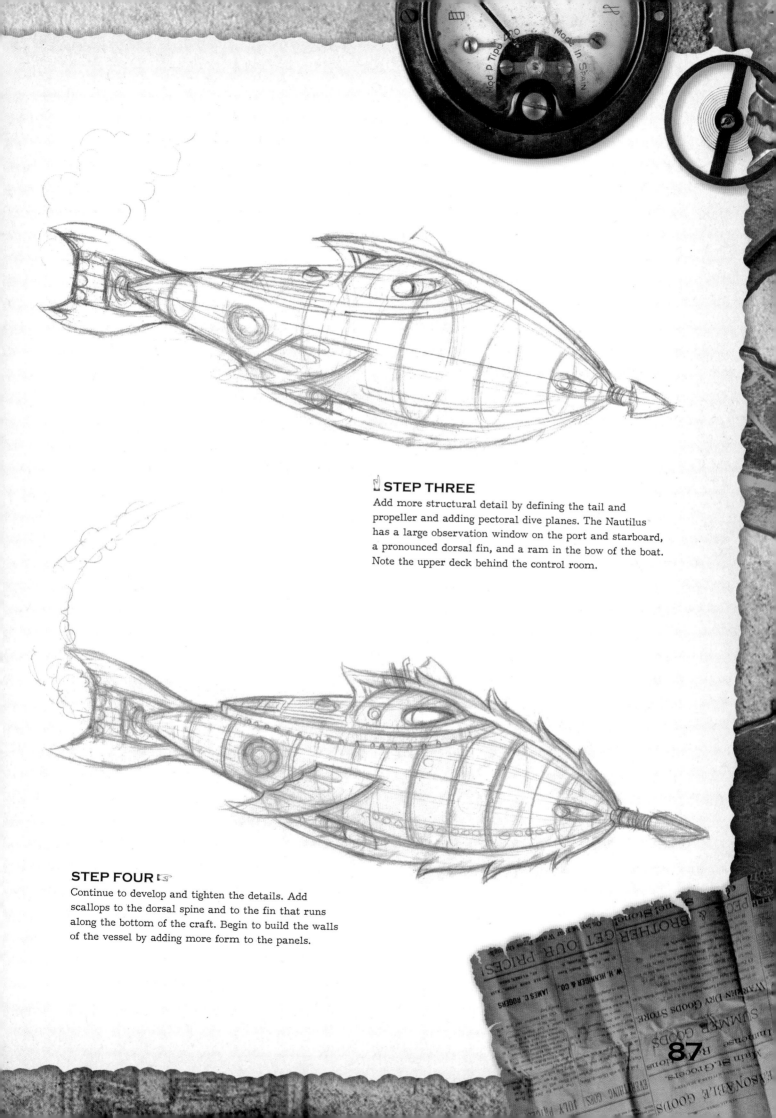

STEP THREE
Add more structural detail by defining the tail and propeller and adding pectoral dive planes. The Nautilus has a large observation window on the port and starboard, a pronounced dorsal fin, and a ram in the bow of the boat. Note the upper deck behind the control room.

STEP FOUR
Continue to develop and tighten the details. Add scallops to the dorsal spine and to the fin that runs along the bottom of the craft. Begin to build the walls of the vessel by adding more form to the panels.

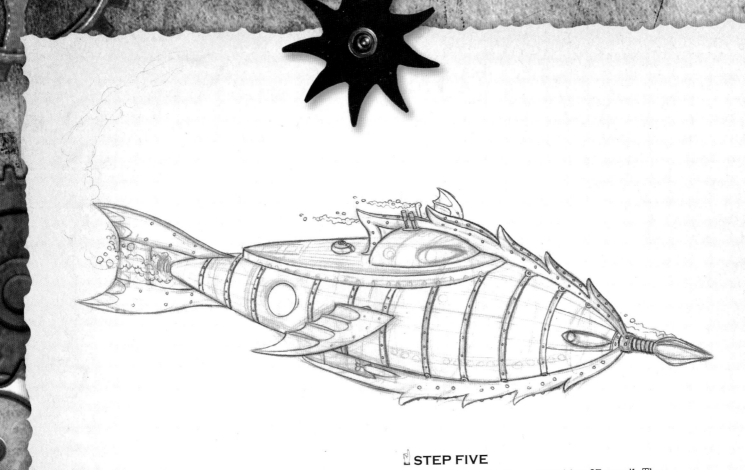

STEP FIVE

Begin to darken the line work with a 2B pencil. Then start refining the outer ribbing of the hull and adding details, such as rivets. Continue to darken the lines, and add snorkels and a periscope to the top of the control cabin.

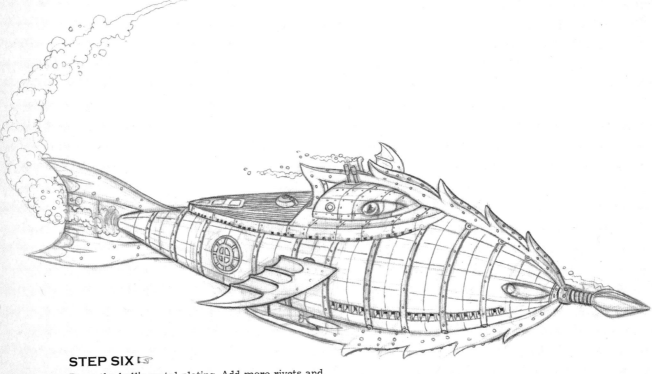

STEP SIX

Draw the hull's metal plating. Add more rivets and small ports for the ballast water along the bottom of the upper deck and the bottom of the hull; then add some trailing bubbles to give the craft a sense of motion.

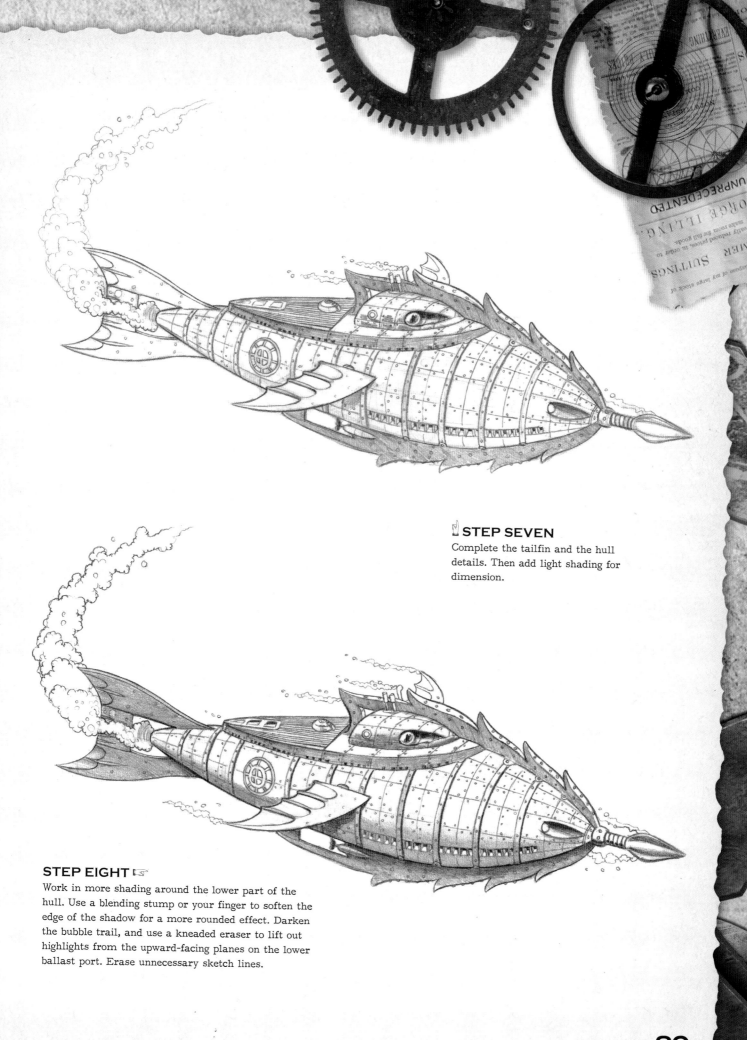

STEP SEVEN

Complete the tailfin and the hull details. Then add light shading for dimension.

STEP EIGHT

Work in more shading around the lower part of the hull. Use a blending stump or your finger to soften the edge of the shadow for a more rounded effect. Darken the bubble trail, and use a kneaded eraser to lift out highlights from the upward-facing planes on the lower ballast port. Erase unnecessary sketch lines.

≈ ZEPPELIN ≈

Explorers who can afford the best in elegance and comfort prefer to travel high in the sky, drifting among the clouds aboard a zeppelin. With plush chambers and high standards of service, the zeppelin's staterooms are five-star accommodations. Not only can such a ship transport mass quantities of weaponry and gear, but its cargo holds can store trophies, including treasure and magnificent beasts.

STEP ONE

Lightly sketch perspective guidelines with a 2H pencil and a ruler. (See "Perspective Basics," page 17). Draw in the rough shape of the balloon and the gondola beneath it.

STEP TWO

Sketch in ellipses, which will help define the volume of the balloon. Rough in the control fins at the rear of the craft, the propeller nacelles mounted at the rear of the gondola, and the eagle's head on the bow.

STEP THREE

This zeppelin has helicopter rotors for vertical lift. Ensure that all the elements of the ship are on the same plane and at the same angle. Add catwalks and access ladders, and lightly outline various windows and doorways. Sketch in ellipses for the remaining rotors, decreasing their sizes as they recede into the distance.

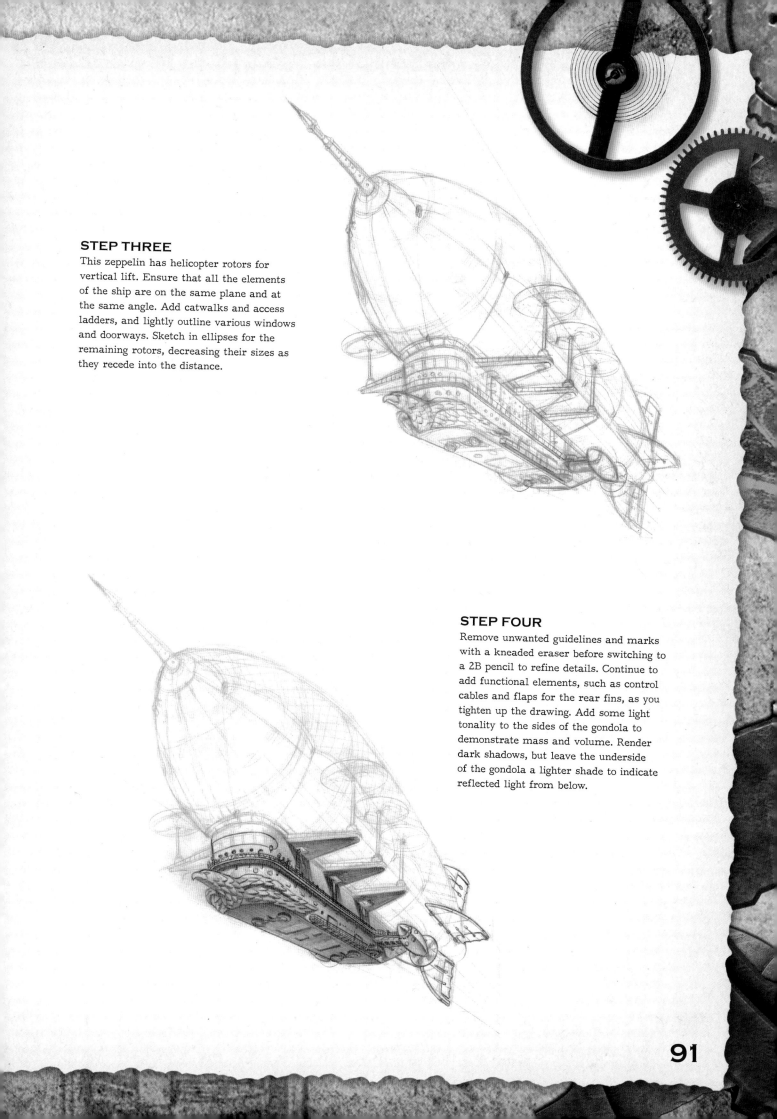

STEP FOUR

Remove unwanted guidelines and marks with a kneaded eraser before switching to a 2B pencil to refine details. Continue to add functional elements, such as control cables and flaps for the rear fins, as you tighten up the drawing. Add some light tonality to the sides of the gondola to demonstrate mass and volume. Render dark shadows, but leave the underside of the gondola a lighter shade to indicate reflected light from below.

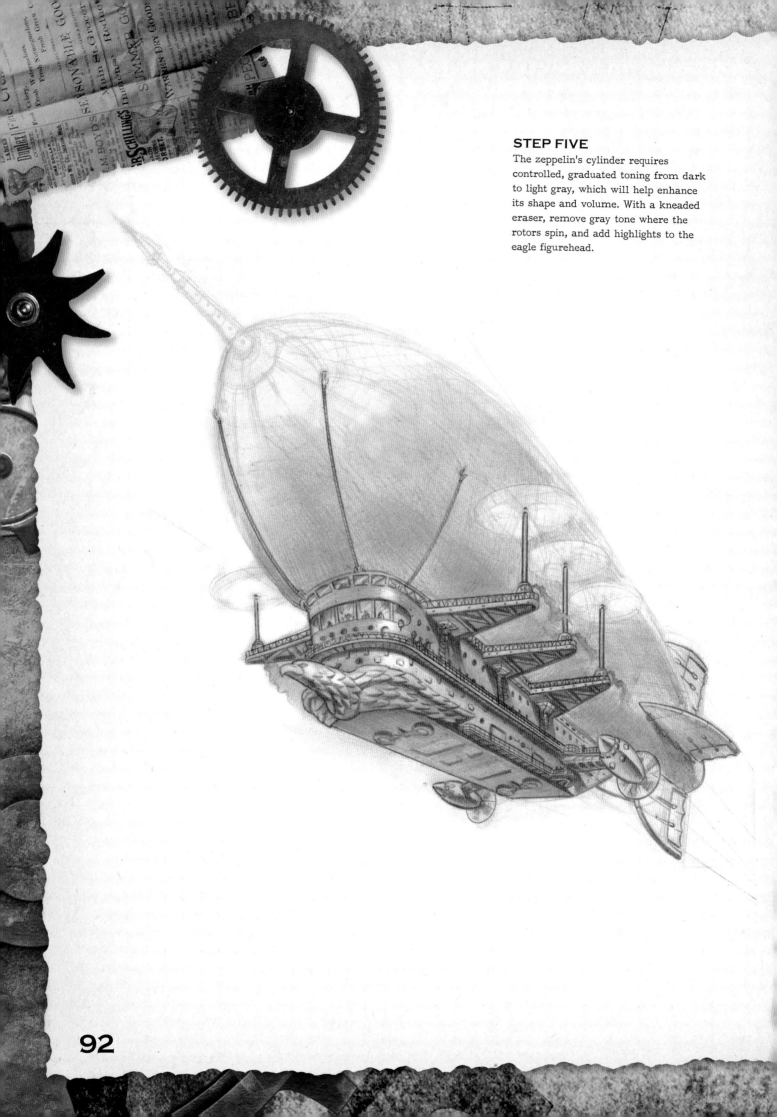

STEP FIVE

The zeppelin's cylinder requires controlled, graduated toning from dark to light gray, which will help enhance its shape and volume. With a kneaded eraser, remove gray tone where the rotors spin, and add highlights to the eagle figurehead.

STEP SIX

Use a kneaded eraser to lift out highlights along the seams that run the length of the balloon, as well as to define the exhaust emitting from below the propellers. Continue to render shading, and finish the docking mast on front of the ship, giving it a metallic appearance. Next, add the netting that drapes over the balloon.

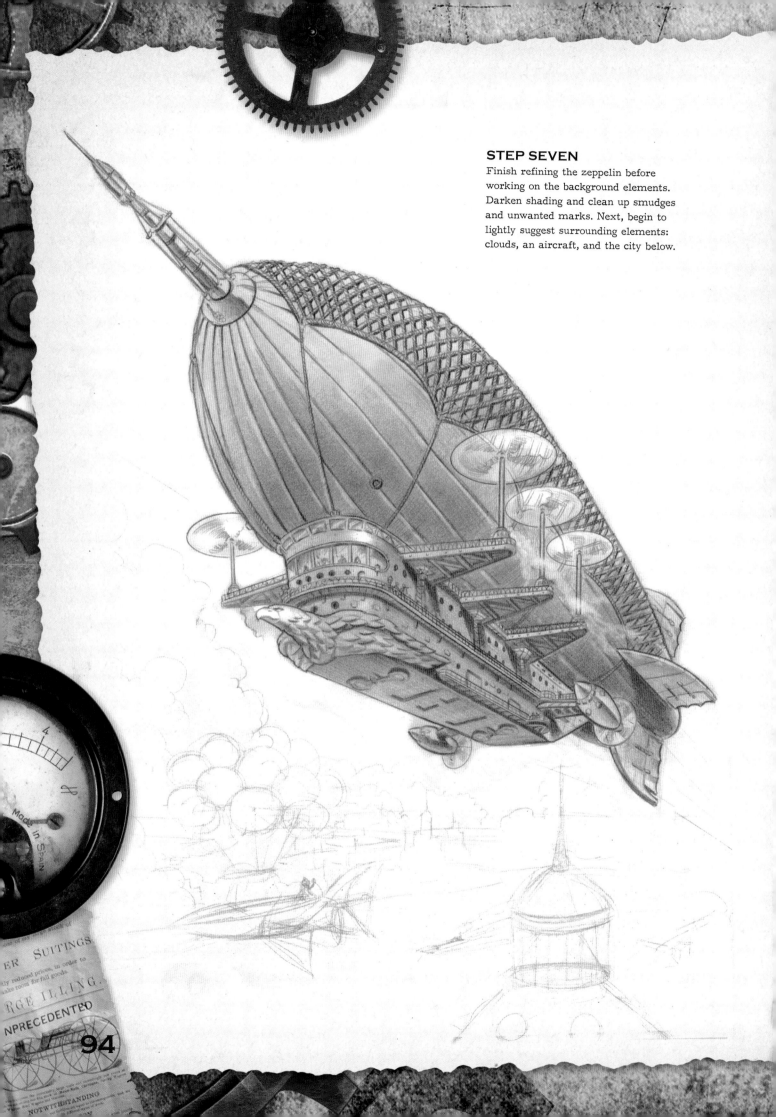

STEP SEVEN

Finish refining the zeppelin before
working on the background elements.
Darken shading and clean up smudges
and unwanted marks. Next, begin to
lightly suggest surrounding elements:
clouds, an aircraft, and the city below.

94

STEP EIGHT

Note that steam, fog, and low-lying clouds partially obscure the cityscape in the background. Use simple marks to suggest buildings in the distance. The roof of a lone tower has been added to the foreground. To create the sky, sprinkle graphite shavings onto the top portion of the drawing; then shake off the excess and use a dry cotton swab to sweep the shavings around in broad strokes. To add clouds, simply remove areas of graphite with a kneaded eraser.

⚜ FLYING GALLEON ⚜

Following the nautical rules of seafaring in the clouds, the flying galleon defies gravity using harnessed electrical power and propulsion. Navigating on the winds, air pirates swashbuckle their way through the air, defending against unimaginable beasts and hijacking any piece of treasure or technology that catches their eye. The crew is trained to use grappling hooks, harpoons, and electrical guns to procure their riches. The cannons mounted to the deck fire electricity rather than cannonballs and will bring down even the most armored of zeppelins in no time. The only insurmountable foe in the sky for the galleon is another equally armed galleon or an air kraken!

STEP ONE

Rough in the ship's hull with a 2H pencil. The shape is complex and curves along two axes, one of which curls upward at both ends. The sides of the ship bow out, making the center of the ship wider than its ends.

STEP TWO
Continue to build up
the details, adding
various rigging for
the sails and the
planking of the ship's
hull, and defining the
side sails and keel.

STEP THREE

Using a 2H pencil, draw the railings, windows, and large coat of arms on the exterior of the half deck. Work out a believable system for lifting and lowering the side sails—details like this will make a drawing more authentic.

STEP FOUR

With the basic elements in place, switch to a softer HB or 2B pencil and begin to trace over the initial sketch, refining the line work and adding more detail. Finish the lower propeller, keel, and rudder. Shade the ship as if it's lit by a single source of light, with reflected light falling in the shadow areas. Even the darkest shadows will quickly fade to a lighter value.

STEP FIVE

Continue to build-up form and add detail, beginning with a dark tone to indicate shadows in the carvings on the half deck. Use a blending stump to soften areas of shading. Carefully draw the railing and the spindles that support it, and begin to develop the rigging and ladders. The mast and the spar in the front of the ship have small bands that depict their cylindrical forms, just as the graduated shading on the side of the hull shows the ship's round, tapering shape.

ADDING COLOR

THERE ARE VARIOUS STYLES OF STEAMPUNK—FROM DARK AND GOTHIC TO WHIMSICAL AND COLORFUL. THE FLYING GALLEON AT THE LEFT WAS PAINTED WITH GOUACHE, A PAINT MEDIUM SIMILAR TO WATERCOLOR. PLAY AROUND WITH DIFFERENT COLOR SCHEMES TO SEE HOW DRASTICALLY THEY CAN ALTER THE MOOD OF YOUR ARTWORK.

STEP SIX

Add layers of shading to enhance the ship's form, and continue to add volume to the sails. With a soft 2B pencil, draw the boiler and enhance the darkest areas of shadow. Lightly sketch in the suggestion of an island in the distance. Finally, use a kneaded eraser to lift out shading above the smokestack to indicate the ship's exhaust.

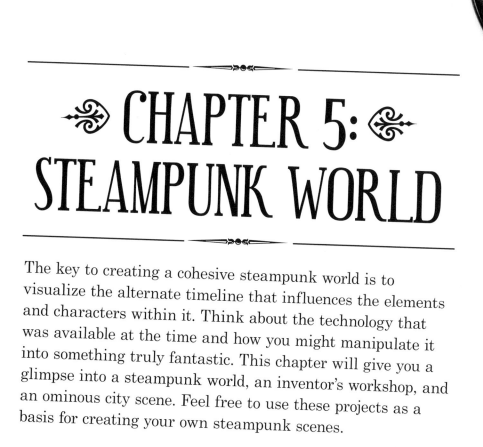

CHAPTER 5: STEAMPUNK WORLD

The key to creating a cohesive steampunk world is to visualize the alternate timeline that influences the elements and characters within it. Think about the technology that was available at the time and how you might manipulate it into something truly fantastic. This chapter will give you a glimpse into a steampunk world, an inventor's workshop, and an ominous city scene. Feel free to use these projects as a basis for creating your own steampunk scenes.

☙ TIME MACHINE ❧

The most common version of this steampunk staple was first described by H. G. Wells in his late-19th-century novel, *The Time Machine*. With elegant brass knobs, and plush, velvety cushions, Wells' machine will take you back in time before it ever leaves the present. Another time-traveling vehicle might take the form of a locomotive similar to the legendary art-deco icon, the Orient Express—chugging through decades spewing coal black smoke. Other time-traveling vessels include automobiles traveling at mach speeds, hand-held weapons that hurl people through time and space, and the iconic police box, or telephone kiosk. But despite the brilliance of a time machine's creator, time travel always leads to unfavorable outcomes.

STEP ONE

Begin by drawing perspective lines with a 2H pencil. Lightly sketch the general shape of the time traveler's machine and laboratory, which is packed with blueprints, charts, and half-finished inventions.

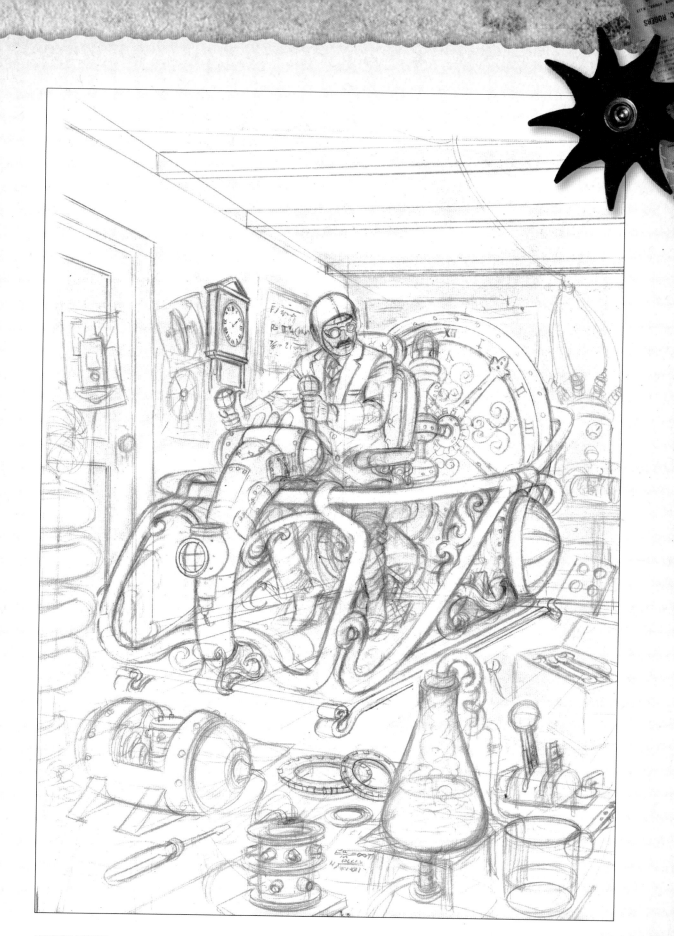

STEP TWO

Refine the structure of your time machine with a 2H pencil, adding decorative metalwork, fine-tuning the disk, and erasing unwanted lines as the drawing progresses. To assist with drawing the figure, pick up details from reference photos.

STEP THREE

Switch to a 2B pencil to refine the time machine's rails, which will help define the volume of the cockpit. Continue to erase sketch lines as the drawing develops and begin to add details to the items in the foreground.

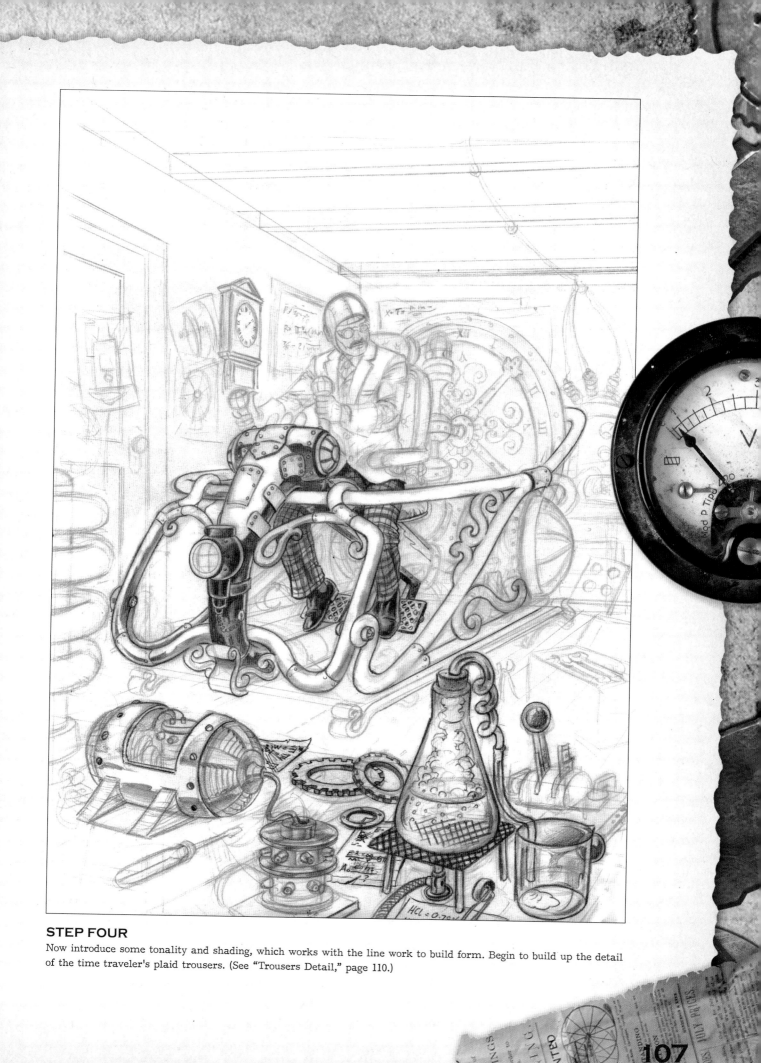

STEP FOUR

Now introduce some tonality and shading, which works with the line work to build form. Begin to build up the detail of the time traveler's plaid trousers. (See "Trousers Detail," page 110.)

STEP FIVE

Continue to use tone to depict volume and texture. Use a kneaded eraser to lift out highlights on the railing, which helps indicate metal shine.

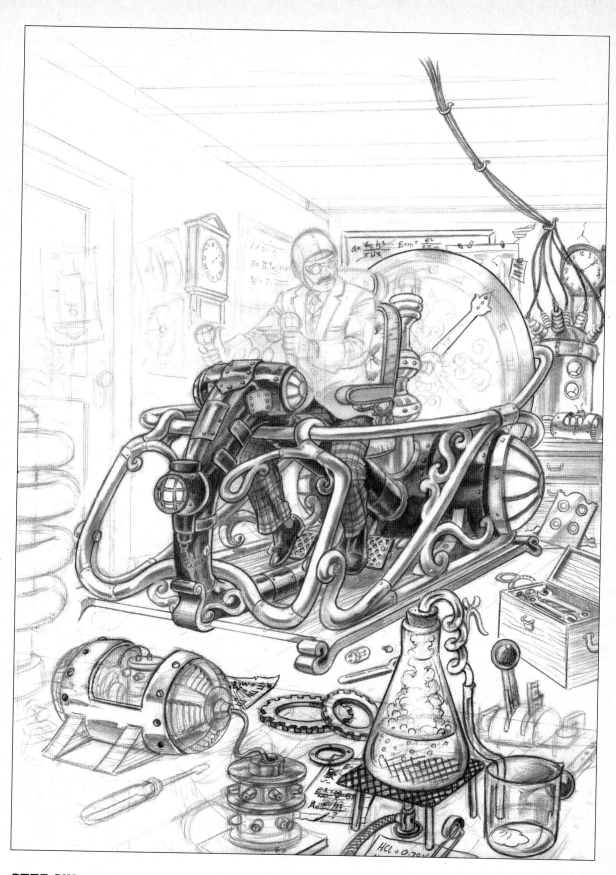

STEP SIX

Next, begin to develop the middle ground. Refine the toolbox and boiler-like contraption behind the time machine, using shading to depict its round form. Contrasting light and dark areas helps create the illusion of depth.

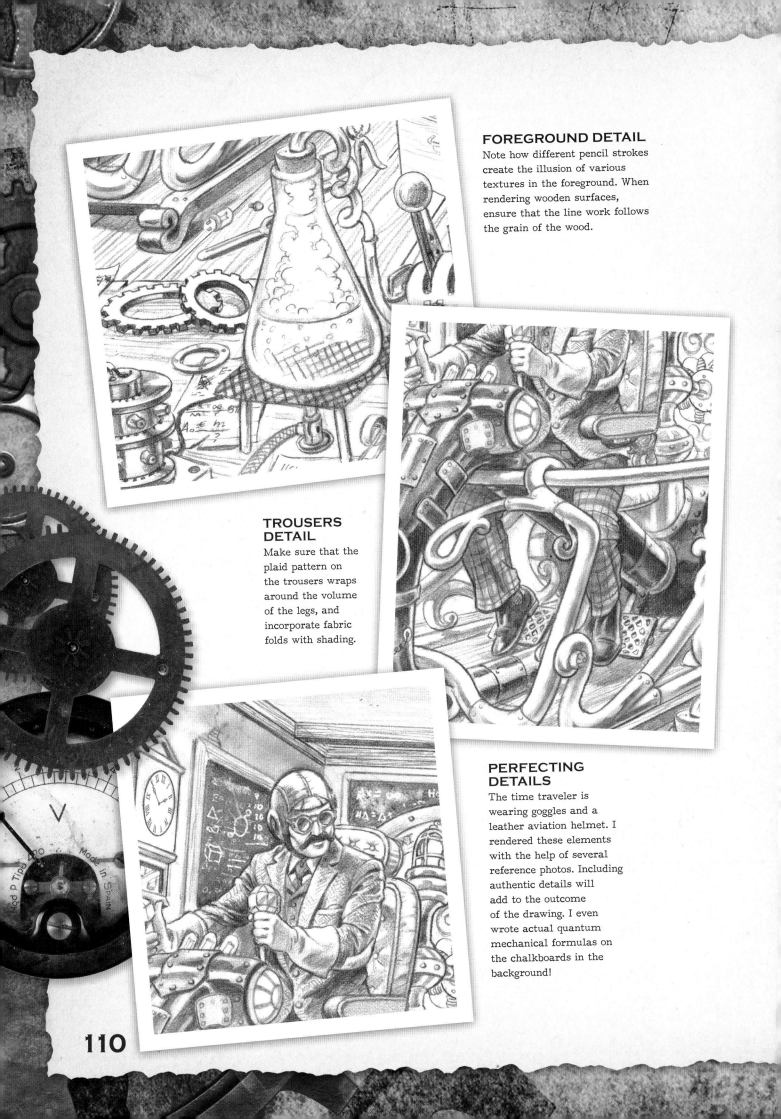

FOREGROUND DETAIL

Note how different pencil strokes create the illusion of various textures in the foreground. When rendering wooden surfaces, ensure that the line work follows the grain of the wood.

TROUSERS DETAIL

Make sure that the plaid pattern on the trousers wraps around the volume of the legs, and incorporate fabric folds with shading.

PERFECTING DETAILS

The time traveler is wearing goggles and a leather aviation helmet. I rendered these elements with the help of several reference photos. Including authentic details will add to the outcome of the drawing. I even wrote actual quantum mechanical formulas on the chalkboards in the background!

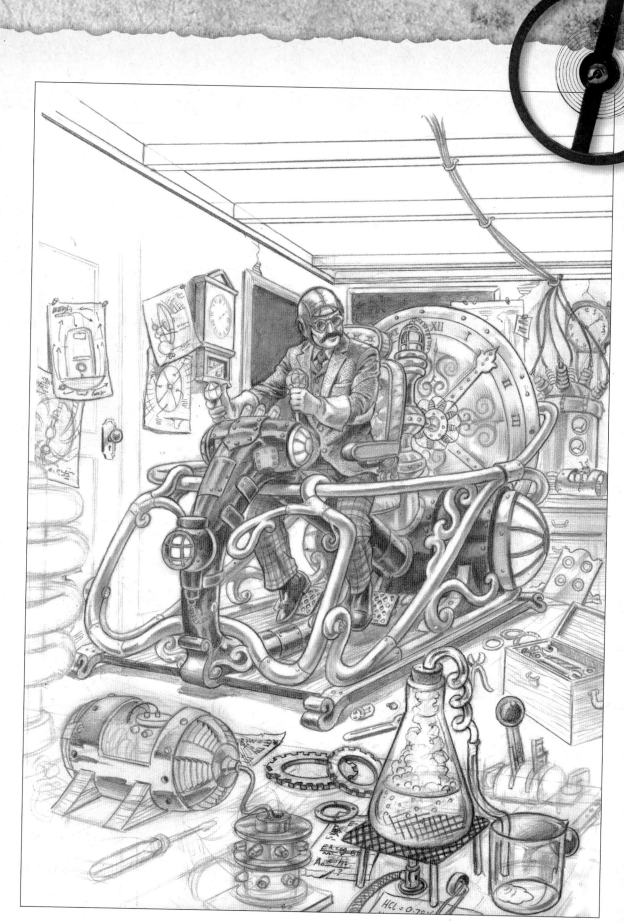

STEP SEVEN

Resolve the various background elements, such as the clocks, blueprints, and chalkboards. Continue to refine and soften the shading.

STEP EIGHT

Add wood textures to the door, ceiling rafters, and floor. This will make the drawing more interesting, add varying degrees of value, and help to define space and form. Finally, render the remaining foreground elements.

STEP NINE

Finish adding the last details, picking out highlights with a kneaded eraser. For additional enhancement, scan the finished drawing into Photoshop. I added a 10% gray tone to the ceiling, floor, and door, and used the digital stylus to write formulas on the blackboards.

❧ STEAM CITY ❧

A steampunk metropolis can take on an array of incarnations. It might take the form of a floating city connected to powerful airships drifting around miles above the earth. It might consist of a vast underwater network of biodomes deep in the ocean, with nautiluses docked in front of every family home. But the most classic image of a steam city calls forth images of building spires that reach upward into the sky, belching smoke and spitting steam. This city rises out of the earth to conquer the land and sky with fantastic contraptions, impressive airships, streets crowded with Victorian-esque men and women, and an aura of mystery lurking in the shadows. This street scene is colored with acrylic paint, an excellent medium for beginners.

BASIC ACRYLIC PAINT PALETTE

- CADMIUM YELLOW
- DEEP BRILLIANT RED
- IVORY BLACK
- LIGHT VIOLET
- PRUSSIAN BLUE
- TITANIUM WHITE
- YELLOW OCHRE
- ACRYLIC GESSO

FIGURE DETAIL
Fill the steam city with Victorian-era characters, using the previous lessons in the book for reference.

LOWER LEVEL DETAIL
Add an element of intrigue to your street scene by drawing walkways on multiple levels.

STEAM CITY DRAWING

Using the previous lessons in the book, draw a steampunk city scene in preparation to add color with acrylic paint. This image relies on the rules of perspective. (See "Perspective Basics," page 17). The street curves and the buildings shrink in size as they recede into the distance. A skyway dominates the skyline in the distance and has a perspective axis running roughly perpendicular to the street. Skyscrapers, airships, flying galleys, and ornithopters complete the scene, and gentle shading adds depth.

STEP ONE

Scan your original drawing and then print it on a laser printer or make a photocopy. Use a pre-sized canvas board, Masonite board, or quarter-inch illustration board as a support. To prepare your surface, create a mixture of half water and half acrylic gesso, and then apply it to your support with a broad brush. Gesso is an acrylic paint medium that will serve as an adhesive for mounting the image to the board. This process can be messy, so protect your work surface with a plastic drop cloth or aluminum foil.

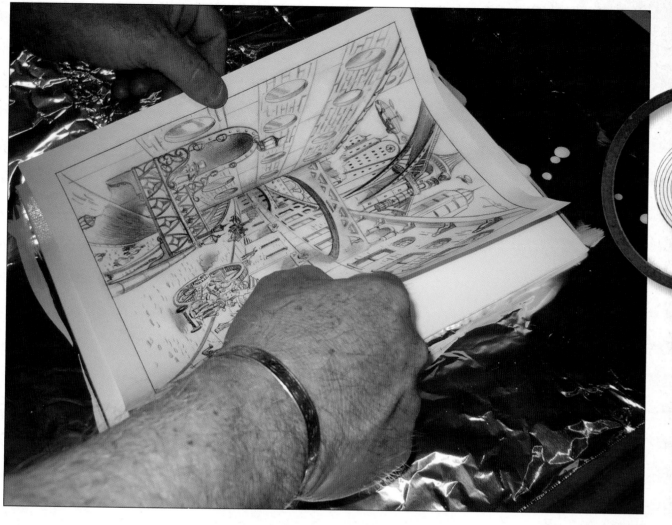

STEP TWO

While the gesso is wet, carefully place the printout of your drawing onto the board, touching the center of the paper to the board first. Press the paper down, moving outward from the center to smooth any wrinkles or trapped air.

STEP THREE

Next, coat the entire surface of the drawing with the same
prepared gesso mixture, painting in directions that will
enhance the forms, but taking care not to overwork it. The
gesso will dry clear and provide a textured work surface
for the application of acrylic paint.

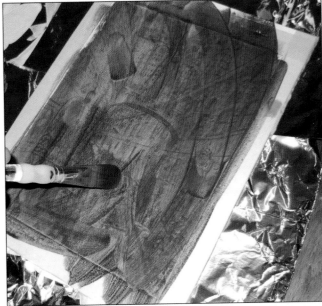

STEP FOUR

Once the gesso has dried completely, create a shade of brick
red by mixing deep brilliant red, yellow ochre, and a small
amount of Prussian blue and ivory black. Use this mixture
to coat the entire surface of the drawing, with brushstrokes
moving in the direction of the buildings and street. This will
serve as the underpainting.

STEP FIVE

Add water to a bit of Prussian blue until the mix is heavily diluted. Use a flat brush to paint a wash over the lower-level street. With the same brush, use light strokes to feather blue into the areas of the buildings that recede into the distance. A few select lanterns placed around the archway on the left will cast a bit of light onto the gloomy scene. Paint in a light wash of cadmium yellow on the footbridge to begin to create this lighting effect.

STEP SIX

With the same wash of Prussian blue used in step five, apply color to the skyway support tower. Then add a touch of titanium white to the wash and paint some highlights onto the iron tower. Mix a bit of light violet into this mixture and apply the wash to the cloud forms behind the airship. Add highlights to the building on the left. Create a mix of black and Prussian blue for the underside and shadow areas of the skyway (Prussian blue is transparent, so add several layers); then add detail to the shadow areas of the building at right. Create a light wash of yellow ochre and titanium white, and paint the right section of the polluted sky and add highlights to the spire behind the skyway. Add a bit more white to this mix, and paint the column of smoke spewing from the smokestack.

STEP SEVEN

With a mix of titanium white, Prussian blue, and light violet, apply color to the clouds for opacity. Then paint the round glass window panes on the left side to indicate reflected light from the lanterns. Next, with black and Prussian blue, enhance the shadow areas beneath the central walkway bridge, in the archway on the left-side building, and underneath the small footbridge.

STEP EIGHT

As the painting progresses, use increasingly opaque paint, which will help to build up and refine form. Create a wash with cadmium yellow, and then lightly feather it around the lantern and wall around the archway. Add yellow ochre and white to make an opaque mixture of yellow, and then paint the surfaces illuminated by the light of the lantern. Paint the surface of the walkway with an opaque mix of yellow ochre, cadmium yellow, and white. Dilute this mixture and apply it to the lanterns at the end of the walkway and to the building above the raised walkway. Add more yellow ochre and cadmium yellow to this mix; then add details to the spire behind the skyway. This building will be bronze, so add some highlights to it using white mixed with cadmium yellow. Use this same mixture to paint the steam factory visible beneath the central walkway.

STEP NINE

Use a wash of yellow to paint the glow of light cast onto the roadway. With a combination of black and Prussian blue, strengthen the shadows beneath the left-side archway and the footbridge. Deepen the shadows on the lower walkway. Mix yellow ochre, cadmium yellow, white, and deep brilliant red to create a lighter version of the brick-wall color for the central walkway. Now define the wrought-iron handrail with a small, pointed brush and a mix of Prussian blue and black. Once it dries, use an opaque mixture of yellow to add highlights. Create a wash from titanium white and Prussian blue, and apply it to the lower-level street to add a sense of mystery. Then, add a bit of black to the brick-red color and paint shadowed areas on the sides of the buildings.

STEP TEN

Apply a bit more blue to the sky and the deepest recesses of the street to create atmospheric perspective in the scene. With the same color, paint details on the cobblestone roadway. Shift to yellow for the highlights on the roadway. Mix a dark brown with the paints on your palette, and begin to add the brickwork on the buildings. Use this mixture to add more shadow to the spire and the farthest building in the distance. With a small, pointed brush, carefully paint the ornithopter's airframe.

STEP ELEVEN

Use an opaque yellow to highlight the interior glow of the lanterns. Mix Prussian blue and light violet into the yellow color. Using diagonal brushstrokes, apply the mixture to indicate light radiating from the windows. Mix a blue-green color and use it to add a patina on various building details, such as the supports beneath the rooflines and the crests above each doorway. Use a blue-gray to initiate the detail on the street vendor on the right side of the scene. With a light value of brick red, create additional brick details throughout.

STEP TWELVE

Begin to define the characters in the scene using the technique described in "Figure Detail" below. After applying a dark wash to each of the figures, start to build them up by adding increasingly lighter values. This is known as painting dark to light. Increase the opacity of the paint to outline the figures for definition.

FIGURE DETAIL

Paint the figures in your scene, beginning with a dark wash of Prussian blue, deep brilliant red, and ivory black for the darkest shadow values.

STEP THIRTEEN

Once every element in the painting has been added, look for areas of shadow that need enhancement, and go over them with an additional dark wash.

❧ CONCLUSION ❧

You now have the knowledge to create your own steampunk universe and illustrate it with all the characters, machines, and gadgets that make the genre truly unique. This journey has taken you from the pages of classic science-fiction literature to steampunk streets brought to life with pencil, paint, and imagination. You have watched your simple sketches develop into detailed depictions of land, air, and oceanic vehicles of grandeur. Now we challenge you to go forth and explore the steampunk world on your own. We hope that your travels are inspiring, and your punk is freshly steamed!

Dr. Grymm's faithful lab assistant, Stitch the Steampug, wearing his time-travel jetpack.